FAMILY W~~ALKS~~

in

CORNWALL

John Caswell

HIGH INTEREST · LOW MILEAGE

Scarthin Books, Cromford, Derbyshire 1992

FAMILY WALKS
in CORNWALL

Family Walks Series
General Editor: Norman Taylor

———————

THE COUNTRY CODE
Guard against all risk of fire
Fasten all gates
Keep dogs under proper control
Keep to paths across farm land
Avoid damaging fences, hedges and walls
Leave no litter
Safeguard water supplies
Make no unnecessary noise
Protect wildlife, wild plants and trees
Go carefully along country roads
Respect the life of the countryside

———————

Published 1992.

Phototypesetting, printing by Higham Press Ltd., Shirland, Derbyshire

ISBN 0 907758 55 X.

Preface

Many years have passed since my first visit to Cornwall when I was introduced to the dramatic cliffs and pounding seas of the north coast. In my teens I enjoyed the sailing opportunities offered by the sheltered waters of St. Mawes and Carrick Roads on the South coast. Subsequently I spent many enjoyable holidays with my family in Cornwall, often camping on one of the delightful sites near the sea. Now that my family have grown up, my wife and I still return to sample the delights of the county, particularly out of season, when the crowds are absent and the traffic is light. Now that we live much nearer to Cornwall we can visit more often that fascinating western peninsula, Penwith, which time has left largely untouched.

About the author

John Caswell is a civil engineer. He spent most of his life in the Midlands but now lives in Somerset surrounded by the wonderful walking country of the south west of England. He has spent much time walking in many parts of Great Britain, sometimes scrambling up the mountains of Wales or the Lake District or skiing in Scotland. His greatest pleasures are walking and music and he makes valiant attempts to extract music from both the piano and the flute, generally not at the same time.

TRINITY HOUSE MUSEUM, PENZANCE

1

CONTENTS

Map of the Area

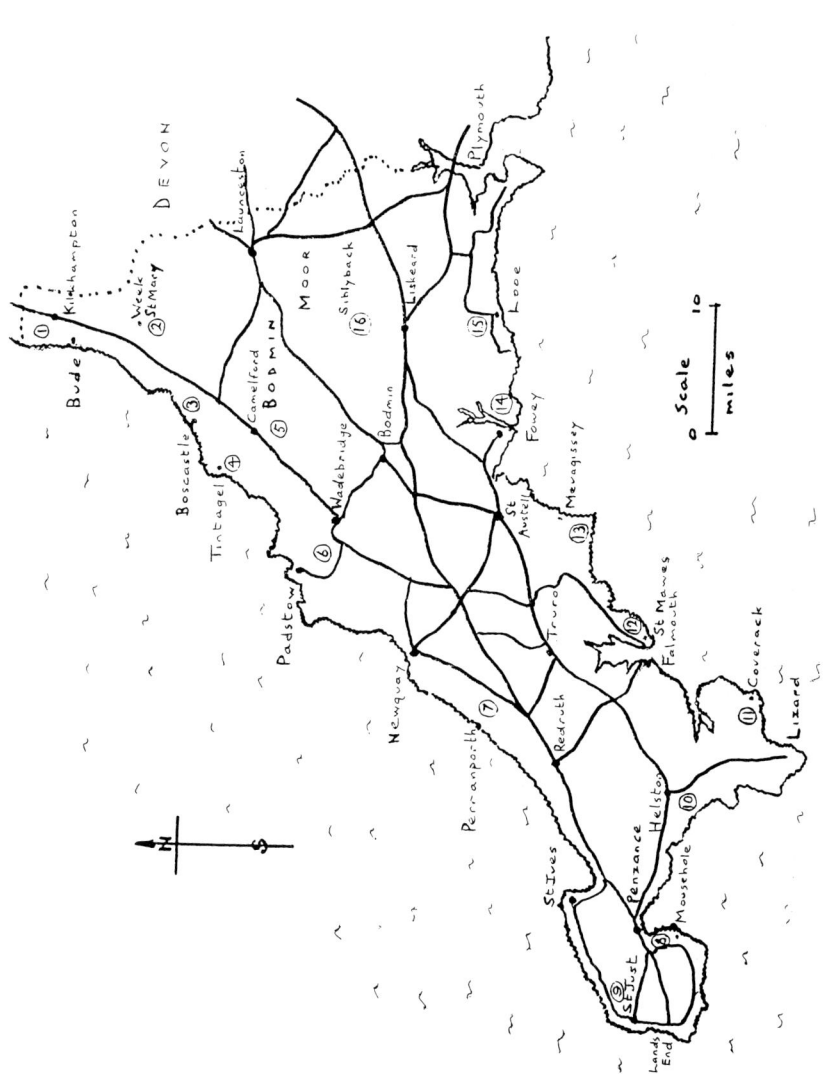

Introduction

Cornwall has many interesting facets and through these walks I hope that you will be able to explore and appreciate some of this beautiful county.

All around the coast the cliffs are magnificent, their twisted formations are a home to a large variety of birds and their tops, covered in gorse, blackthorn and bramble, shelter a fantastic collection of flora and fauna. Many of the walks take in these coastal stretches for part of the route and are especially delightful in spring and early summer when the flowers greet the walker around every corner. The banks and hedges along the inland walks are equally delightful and an early holiday when the primroses and violets abound and before the more vigorous plants overtake the smaller varieties can be most rewarding. It is then that you can park easily in the most popular of beauty spots, wander freely and enjoy the colour at its best.

A major contrast between north and south Cornwall is to be found on the coast where the Atlantic surf pounds on to the northern beaches whereas the south facing beaches receive a gentler tide. On the south coast, as land masses have moved up and down, the ancient river valleys have been flooded by the sea and now, at the River Fal, Helford, Fowey and Looe, these inlets offer splendid walks where sea meets the land but are much more sheltered than the open coast walks. Within such a short distance there are major contrasts between the large resorts such as Newquay and the tiny inlet of Tintagel with its castle and legends of King Arthur.

Nearly everywhere there is evidence of past mining activity both inland and along the cliffs and here and there the odd chimney still reaches skyward to remind you of the days when lead, tin and copper played an important part in the county's economy. The county's connection with mining is epitomized in the Museum of Mining at Cambourne where mineral specimens from all over the world are displayed. It was also in this area, through the work of the College at Cambourne, that the most recent attempts were made to harness the heat of the granite in the earth's crust to provide useful power.

Granite forms the backbone of the county and where it has forced its way near to the surface it has been mined for many generations and used for innumerable things in countless places. The decomposed feldspar which is called china clay or kaolin is the other major geological feature of Cornwall. The tips around St. Austell are visible for a long distance and the material is carried away in a procession of trains, lorries and boats.

Bodmin Moor forms a major feature of east Cornwall. I have described walks at the edge of the moor from where you can readily explore further into the moor if you so wish, although such open country doesn't lend itself to written directions.

The county has been far less disturbed and exploited than most other counties of England and for this reason there are many neolithic and bronze age remains to be seen. The far west in particular has a fascinating collection of remains and the small fields surrounded by low stone walls have been cultivated since the Iron Age.

Many of the churches are dedicated to Early Christians who landed here and founded their cells and even today there are many holy wells in the area. Several walks include churches that are worth a pause for a look inside.

Literature

Many books have been written about Cornwall or based on its unique character, and below I mention a few which may enhance your holiday in the area.

In the far west of Cornwall, in the Penwith peninsula extending to Land's End, there are many remains left by the pre-historic inhabitants. Although one of the walks in this book covers some of these remains, the book *Journey to the Stones* written by Ian Cooke, provides a series of walks designed to visit most of these sites. It gives a brief outline of the way in which society changed during the prehistoric period into the Dark Ages.

The Sun and the Serpent, written by Hamish Miller and Paul Broadhurst, is an investigation into Earth Energies by tracking one of the worlds most famous ley lines. The line runs from the far west tip of Cornwall and through such sacred sites as Glastonbury Tor and Avebury. By following the line in Cornwall you will find many interesting historical and religious sites hidden away in the most unlikely corners. You may be tempted to follow the energies yourself using a pair of divining rods which you can use on the stone circles on some of the walks in this book.

Jamaica Inn which stands on Bodmin Moor (at Bolventor on the A30) was immortalised by Daphne du Maurier in her novel of that name. Read it for an insight into the life of Cornwall in bygone times and visit the old coaching inn which also has a Daphne du Maurier room.

Place names

As the Saxons invaded, they forced the Britons to retreat to the west and both Cornwall and Wales became outposts of the Celtic people and their language, thus many place names today are derived from the Celtic language. The following is a list of some common place names.

5

Brea, Bray	Hill	Gwyn	White
Car, Caer	Fort	Pons, Pont	Bridge
Carn	Rock	Porth	Harbour, Bay
Chy, Che	House	Tre, Trev	Farm, Home
Du, Dhu	Black	Treth	Beach
Eglos, Lan	Church	Whel, Wheal	Mine

Public Transport

There is still a rail service to the west of Cornwall although many of the lines to the coast have been closed. The principal stations on the main line to Plymouth and the rest of England are Penzance, Cambourne, Redruth, Truro, St. Austell, Par, Lostwithiel, Bodmin, Liskeard and Saltash. Branches run to St. Ives, to Falmouth, to Newquay, and to Looe, while Barnstaple in Devon is the nearest rail terminus for Bude and North East Cornwall.

Long distance coaches serve many parts but several areas are very inaccessible if you rely on regular public transport.

In relation to the walks themselves, there are very few regular bus services which would be of any interest to the walker except in the following areas. Several routes cover the Penzance/Land's End/St. Ives peninsula and Helston/Lizard area. Truro is linked with Newquay and Perranporth and also with Falmouth. (Falmouth is linked to St. Mawes by ferry). Fowey is linked with Par and St. Austell and a bus links St. Austell to Mevagissey.

Padstow, Wadebridge and Bodmin are linked. Buses run from Boscastle to Tintagel. Tintagel is linked with Plymouth, Camelford and Bodmin (Bodmin Railway Station is a long way from the town centre). Buses link Exeter station with Bude from where a bus runs to Kilkhampton.

Under current legislation buses are either provided as a normal commercial operation where it is profitable, or provided as a service subsidized by the County Council and operated by the person putting in the lowest (generally) tender to operate them. Services are in a state of flux and only County Councils can provide current details of the many operators in the area. Enquiries should be directed to the County Council at Truro although local tourist offices can (sometimes not open all year round) offer advice where appropriate.

The walks

All walks have been chosen to suit the needs of families although they are equally enjoyable by walkers of any age or disposition, in groups or alone. There is plenty to occupy the family en-route, rivers, streams, woods, picnic spots, old forts, stone circles, rocks or beaches. All are in beautiful surroundings, with a wealth of flora and fauna.

There are variations suggested for most of the basic routes and a glance at the maps may introduce other possibilities, such that a large number of excursions can be made in addition to the basic circuits.

If you carry the right food and drink in your rucksack, then even the longest walks become shorter - whatever the weather.

Pace and timing

A group of fast walkers rarely average more than 2½ miles an hour allowing for gates, stiles, and pauses to appreciate the scenery. Young children will manage much less and hill climbing will add further time.

Clothing

It is difficult to give specific advice on the best type of clothing for these walks as they range from a seaside stroll to the rigours of open moorland. Though most will be done in summer, I am sure that some walkers will sample the delights of walking in winter and spring when the county is just as attractive and much less crowded.

Comfortable footwear is essential and it should be waterproof. Farm tracks and open moorland can be equally waterlogged, especially in wet weather. However many will find stout trainers adequate for short walks in dry weather. Thin soles offer less protection against rough surfaces although some walking boots may be too stiff or heavy. Try a variety before buying and preferably wear two pairs of socks, one thick and one thin. Sandwich bags worn over socks can help if boots are leaky.

Waterproofs range from the cheap non-breathing materials to those claimed to be fully permeable to water vapour and impermeable to rain, thus avoiding the problem of sweat condensing inside. Opinions vary widely on the efficiency of these fabrics. The non-breathable type are in general cheaper and lighter.

Warmth is essential, especially on the exposed walks on cliff tops or open moorland. This can best be achieved with several thin layers topped with a windproof layer. Most heat is lost through the head and a woolly hat is a great asset. A pair of woollen gloves can be a boon on cold days - remember the wind chill factor on windy days.

Spare clothing can be wrapped in a plastic bag (to keep dry) and carried in a rucksack.

Symbols used on the route maps

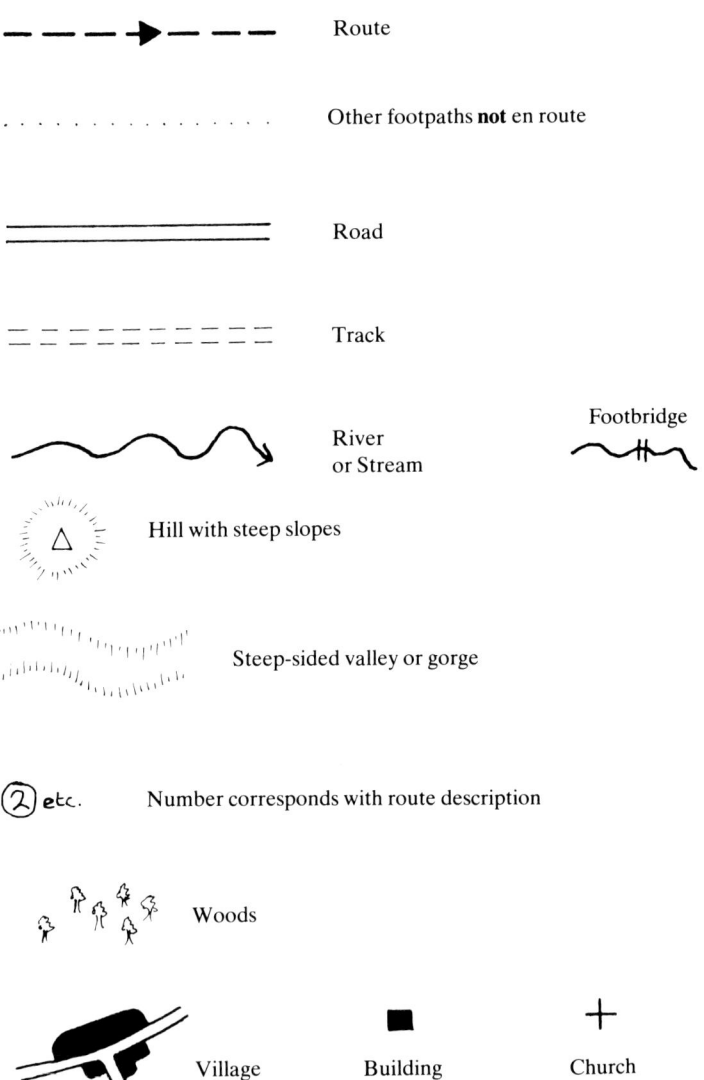

— — — ➤ — — —   Route

. . . .   Other footpaths **not** en route

════════════   Road

━ ━ ━ ━ ━ ━ ━ ━ ━   Track

River or Stream

Footbridge

Hill with steep slopes

Steep-sided valley or gorge

② etc.   Number corresponds with route description

Woods

Village   Building   Church

8

Route 1 3 miles

(shorter variation 2 miles)

Coombe Valley

Outline   Duckpool ~ Coombe Valley ~ Duckpool.

Summary   A pleasant stroll starting on the sea shore and walking through farmland and woodland to return alongside a lovely stream.

Attractions   This is a short stroll to sample the delights of Cornish rambles and to offer a welcome break to the weary travellers just after crossing the border into Cornwall. Duckpool is the name which now attaches to the small rocky inlet set beneath the headland of Steeple Point, near the village of Kilkhampton. After skimming a few of the flat stones into the sea which have come from the shales in the cliffs in the vicinity, you may gain the higher ground and get your first panoramic view of the cliffs and sea. In the woods there is a Nature Trail, a picnic area, and plenty of scope for hide and seek. At the edge of the wood is the former watermill and the path passes close to where the two mill leates meet which used to drive the mill wheel. Note the carved stone inscription on the Duckpool Bridge, an old road bridge over the river. It records that in the year of human redemption 1836, King William the Fourth gave £20 towards the funds which were raised by public subscription, "Fear God, Honour the King".

The church at Kilkhampton has some superb carved oak pews and bench ends, which date from 1567, and an organ originally built in 1680 which has most of the original pipework.

Refreshments   There are inns and refreshments at Morewenstow and Kilkhampton. Bude is nearby, with a wide selection of refreshments.

Route 1

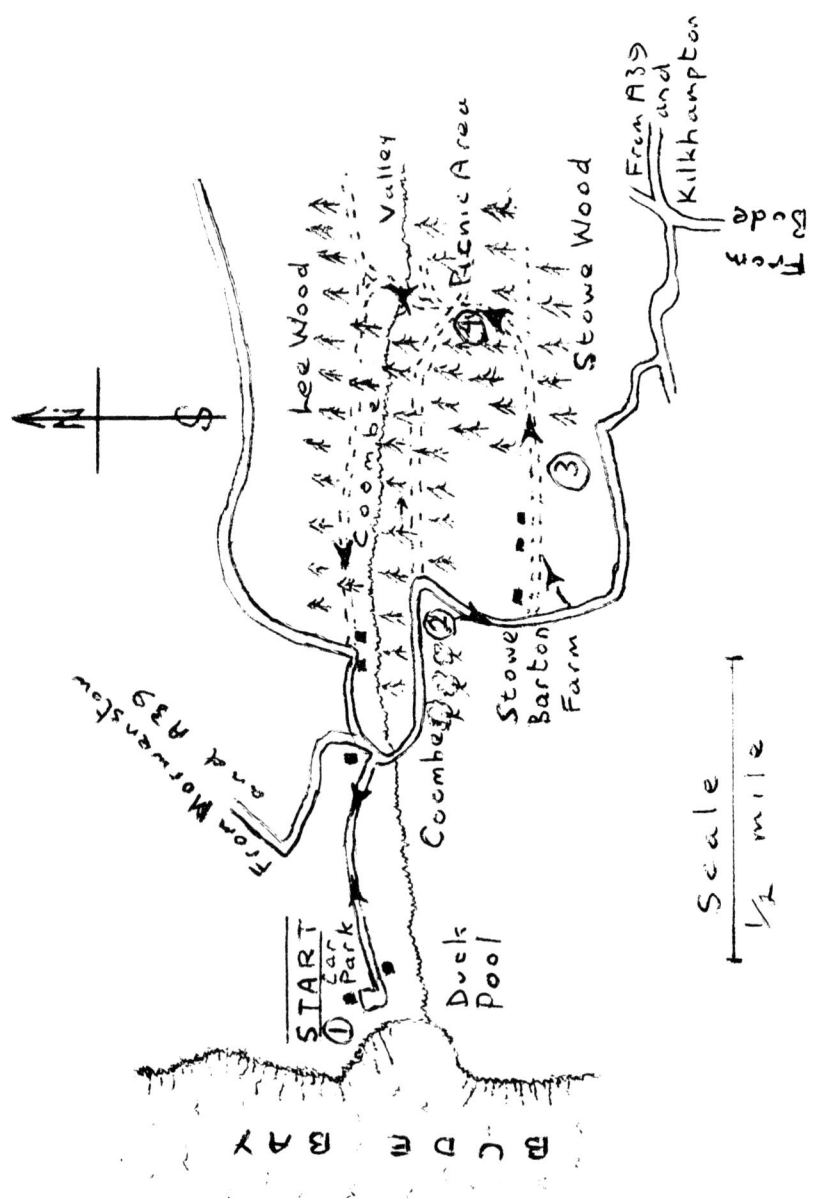

10

Route 1

3 miles
(shorter variation 2 miles)

Coombe Valley

START   *From the car park/toilets on the sea front at Duckpool, near Kilkhampton. (G.R. 201117).*

ROUTE

1. *From the car park, walk back along the lane along which you have just driven and turn right at the first junction. Pass over the bridge and follow the lane as it bends left and climb into the woods.*
2. *At the hairpin bend follow the road sharply to the right to pass Stowe Barton Farm. At the end of the high wall turn left into the field through the field gate, and walk diagonally across the field towards the buildings of Stowe Barton, but aiming for the right hand end of the block of buildings, to join the farm track. Follow the track, passing some houses on the left. At the end of the houses maintain the same direction along a grassy track to enter a valley.*
3. *Cross a stile leading down into the woods and follow the broad track ahead downhill, ignoring the first right branch.*
4. *At the picnic area take the right fork to cross a stream and maintain roughly the same direction (ignoring the sharp right turn and also the next right fork). Continue (slightly downhill) as the forest track swings then crosses over a concrete bridge to reach another wide junction. Here, continue bearing to the left and follow a straight track with the stream below you on the left to reach the tarmac road at the old mill stream. Join the tarmac road and continue in the same direction. Turn right just before the river bridge, towards the sea and the starting point.*

SHORTER VARIATION

At point 2 enter the woods and follow the valley with the stream on the left for ½ mile, then turn left over the stream (at point 4) and return on the other side of the valley.

NOTE

Kilkhampton stands on the A39 main road. The lanes between Kilkhampton and Duckpool are very narrow and it is best to approach the starting point from Morwenstow direction i.e. from the north along the coast road. Morwenstow is signed off the A39 about 3 miles north of Kilkhampton.

11

HELSTON

Route 2

3 miles
(shorter variation 2 miles)

Week St. Mary

Outline   The Church ~ Swannacott Wood ~ Week Green ~ The Church.

Summary   A stroll around and about a Cornish village.

Attractions   This walk is a contrast to the many others in this book which are near the exposed sea cliffs or towards the higher open moorland. It is best reserved for those very windy days when the more exposed routes are not attractive. It is an opportunity to stroll around a village and watch it at work and play. There is plenty of opportunity to see the sheep, cattle or horses in the fields. Pause a while in the woods where the route crosses the stream, study the wide variety of plants in this sheltered damp location and note the variety of trees which form the hedges on the walk.

It is a historically interesting village. Look to the left after point 2 and you will see the flat topped circular hill which is Ashbury. This was a pre-historic fortified "bury", and the remains of the earthworks surrounding it are still visible. There was a church here in Celtic times. Over the entrance to the church is an ancient sundial and inside, notice the elaborately carved choir stalls. This is where lightning disproves the theory that it never strikes twice in the same place as the high tower has been struck several times. Don't worry now though as they have fitted lightning conductors! Near the church are the remains of a Norman castle; and a grammar school or college was founded here in the 16th century. John Wesley visited the village several times and preached in the church.

Refreshments   There is a Country House Hotel in the village with a tea garden, and also an inn.

Route 2

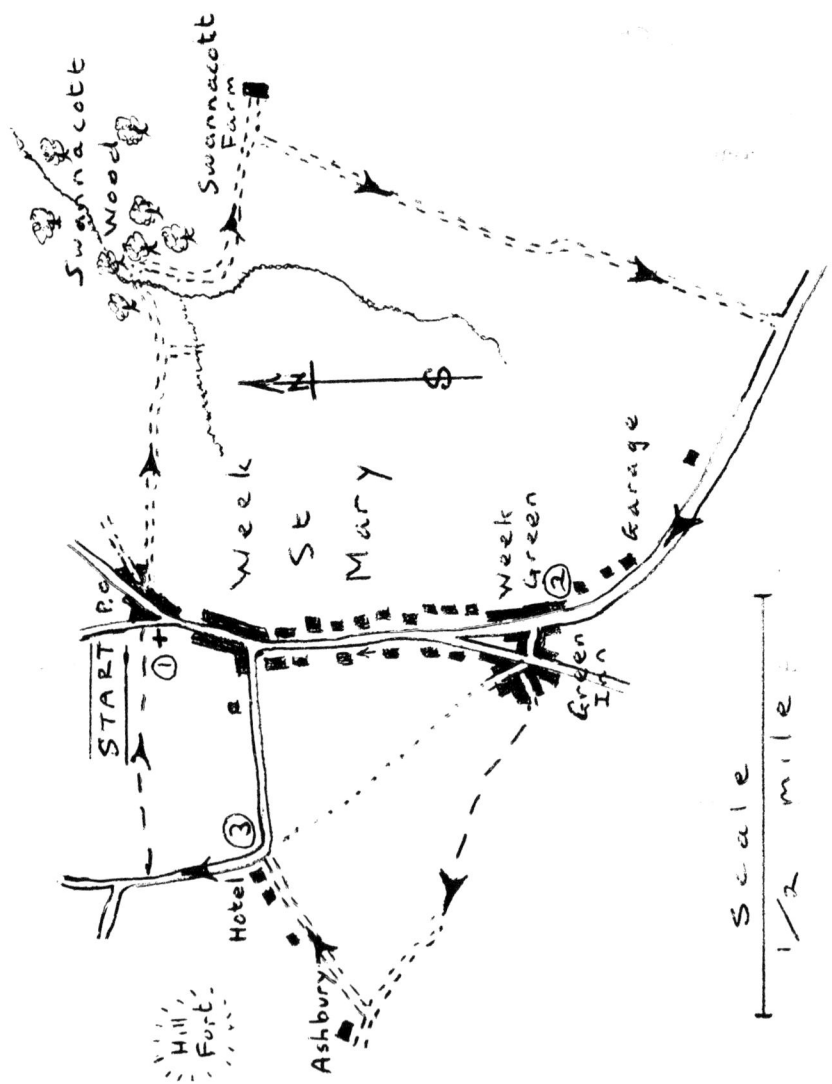

Route 2

3 miles
(shorter variation 2 miles)

Week St. Mary

START   *At the car park area adjoining the village church (G.R. 238978).*

ROUTE

1. *With your back to the church gate bear left to pass the Post Office and then turn left along the main street. After about 100 yards two tracks fork off to the right. Take the track which is furthest to the right. Follow the track as it descends (ignoring the wide fork to the right) to reach a bridge in the woods. Cross the bridge and bear right to follow a lane which meets a tarmac farm track at Swannacott Farm after about ¼ mile. Turn right to reach the main road after about 1 mile, and turn right along the main road. After passing the garage on the right, turn next left at Week Green.*

2. *Pass in front of The Green Inn at Week Green, cross the road, and follow the track on the opposite side of the junction for a few yards only. Turn left between the bungalow and the barn and follow the track which shortly bears to the right. Follow this track as it becomes a field path, maintaining the same direction, and then becomes a track again with hedges on both sides.*
   At Ashbury, turn right to follow the farm drive to the road.

3. *Turn left along the tarmac road and, just before the next road junction, turn right over the stile into the field. Keep the hedge on your right and walk down the field, cross the stream, and climb up towards the church, passing through the gate which you will notice on the right in the church boundary.*

SHORTER VARIATION

At point 2, do not turn left, but carry on ahead to follow the main street to the church.

NEAR BOSCASTLE

16

Route 3
Boscastle

Outline Boscastle ~ River Valency ~ Minster Church ~ Bottreaux Castle ~ Boscastle.

Summary A very pleasant ramble through the lovely wooded valley and hillside and exploring the site of an old castle.

Attractions The walk alongside the river is a delight for all the family with all the usual attractions of the waterside and woodland combined. The ground around Minster church is full of daffodils and bluebells. Boscastle is one of several places to have a legend relating to church bells which were lost due to shipwreck and which you can still hear ringing beneath the sea. It certainly is a narrow harbour with a tortuous entrance, but it is very dramatic, set beneath the towering cliffs, and well worth the small diversion from the walk. There are some very picturesque houses to see as you descend the old main street, before diverting to the site of Bottreaux Castle. A traditional floral dance is performed weekly in Boscastle.

Refreshments There is a wide choice of refreshments in Boscastle.

BOSCASTLE

17

Route 3

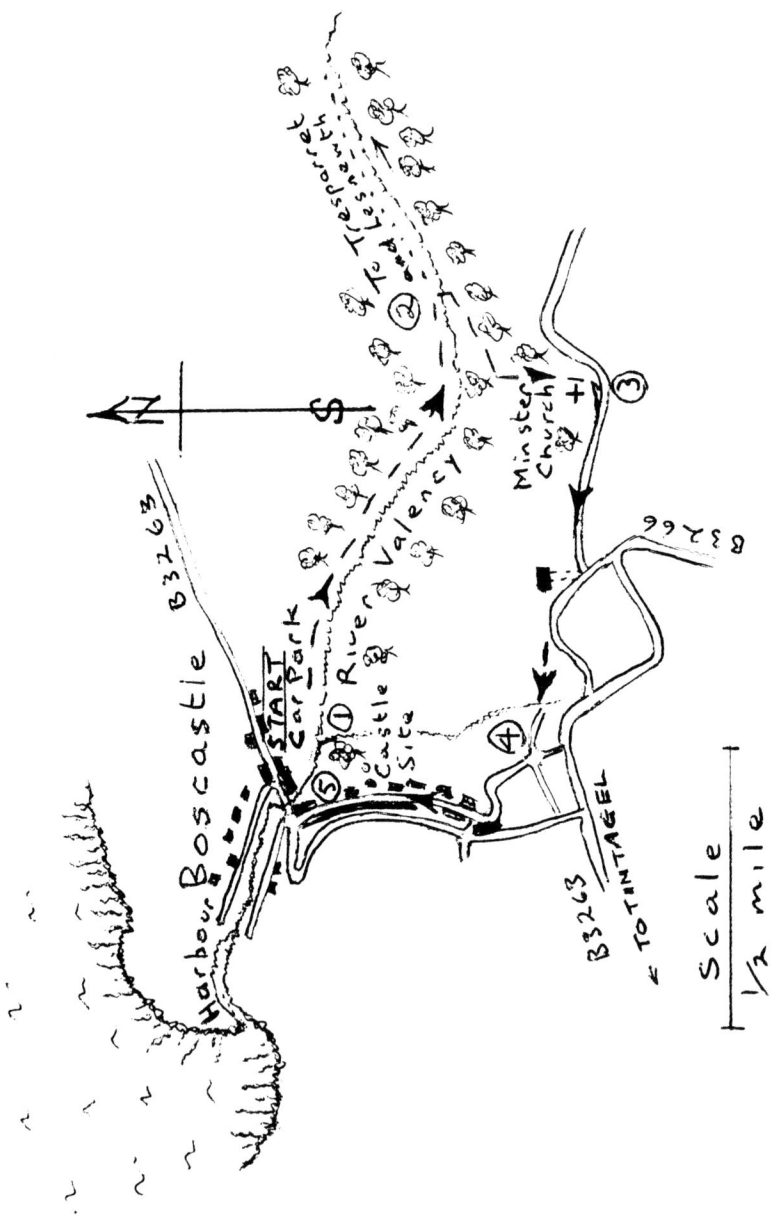

Route 3

3 miles

Boscastle

START   *From the car park/toilets adjoining the main street at Boscastle (G.R. 100913).*

ROUTE

1. *Walk through the small gap at the far end of the car park and bear left to follow the riverside path as far as a footbridge.*

2. *Turn right over the footbridge and follow the path which rises up through the woods to meet the tarmac road at Minster Church. (To visit the church, follow the path which drops to the right just before reaching the road).*

3. *Turn right to follow the road, and go right at the junction. Where the road bends left, cross the stile straight ahead. Bear slightly to the left to descend towards and cross the stream and join a tarmac drive.*

4. *When the drive meets the road turn right down the old main street of Boscastle. After about 200 yards look for the sign to the site of the castle (right). From the castle return to the road and follow it down to the bottom of the hill.*

5. *Take a diversion to the Harbour on the left, (and maybe also the exhibition of illusion and holograms) before returning to the car park, which is just around the corner.*

VARIATION

If time permits you may extend the walk along the valley and then follow the road to Tresparret, before rejoining the circuit at point 2.

BOSSINEY HAVEN

20

Route 4

4 miles
(shorter variations 3 and 3½ miles)

Tintagel

Outline   Tintagel ~ St. Nectan's Glen ~ St. Piran's Well ~ Tintagel.

Summary   A very interesting walk through delightful woodland to a waterfall and then visiting a picturesque chapel, a Roman milestone, and old well, and some Bronze Age carvings.

Attractions   Tintagel is one of the renowned sites of Dark Age Britain reputed to be the birthplace of King Arthur. Pottery made in North Africa in Roman times and pottery imported from the Mediterranean area in the Dark Ages has been found here. It is a village which is full of the legends of Arthur and his Knights. The interesting ruins of the castle dominate the little harbour and are well worth a visit. On the nearby promontory are the remains of cells of an ancient monastery. Check the state of the tide before you set off and then decide the best time to see Merlin's Cave below the castle. The Old Post Office is in the charge of the National Trust and en-route you can also drop into the mineral museum or King Arthur's Hall to see the exhibits.

To see the waterfall you must pay an entrance fee, but the walk along St. Nectan's Glen is a delight, even if you decide not to go in to see the waterfall itself. In the glen King Arthur's Knights prayed before setting out to seek the Holy Grail.

St. Piran's chapel could very likely be a relic of 6th century christianity. St. Piran is the patron saint of Cornwall, and in the east wall of the chapel is a stained-glass lancet window showing St. Piran standing at the top of a rocky valley, presumably the one you will walk through. On a window ledge is a pre-Norman lamp shaped in stone. Nearby, in the nursery garden is a Roman milestone. There are several such stones in Cornwall but none show any mileage, they were erected to record the end of the project and the name of the emperor.

Between the main road and the sea, as you reach a group of derelict buildings, after crossing the bridge by the trout farm café, look carefully at the rock face to discover the bronze-age carvings depicting a maze.

Refreshments   There is a large choice of refreshments in Tintagel. There is a café at the waterfall and another by the trout farm between the main road and Bossiney Haven.

Route 4

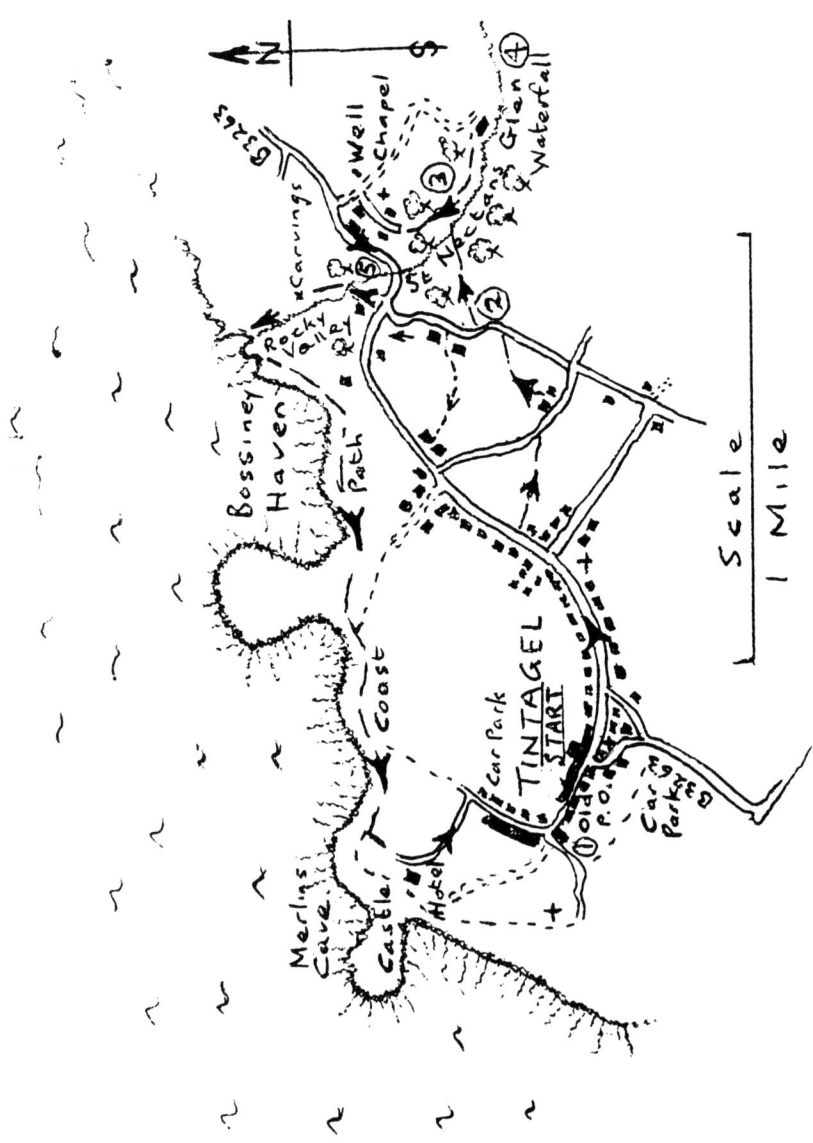

22

Route 4

4 miles

(shorter variations 3 and 3½ miles)

Tintagel

START   *From the Old Post Office (National Trust property) in the main street of Tintagel. (G.R. 056884). There are several car parks nearby.*

ROUTE

1. *From the Old Post Office walk uphill away from the sea. After passing the third road on the right you reach open fields on the right and a stile. Cross the stile and bear half left to cross the 3 field boundaries and stone stiles consistently maintaining the same direction to reach the lane. Cross the stile here and keep the same direction, walking up the lane to reach the buildings on the left. Turn left, keeping the second house on your right, to cross a stile beyond the house. Walk along the field keeping the hedge on your left to reach a stile in the hedge ahead which leads on to the lane. Turn left and walk along the lane for about 200 yards to a bend.*

2. *At this bend, turn right over a stile. Cross the field diagonally to walk downhill and cross a stile to enter the woods. Follow the path down to the stream and cross the bridge.*

3. *Turn right and walk to the waterfall café.*

4. *Return from the café to the bridge and pass the bridge, keeping the stream on your left, to reach the tarmac lane which leads to St. Piran's Chapel and Well. Turn left; and left again at the main road. Walk carefully along the main road to cross the stream at Rocky Valley and turn right at the next gate.*

5. *Follow the drive and path past the café, over the bridge to the site of the carvings, and to the sea at Bossiney Haven. Turn left and follow the Coast Path. As you approach Tintagel along the path you will see a large hotel near the cliffs. Take the path which leads to the left of the hotel grounds to reach the tarmac road, and follow the road to the Old Post Office.*

SHORTER VARIATIONS

A. *At point 2 you may go a few yards further around the bend and turn left through the farmyard to follow the path to the main road. Turn left at the main road and return to the start.*

B. *At point 2 do not enter the field but follow the lane to the main road and turn right to point 5. This avoids the main road between point 5 and the chapel as this road has no footpath.*

ST. PIRAN'S WELL (Route 4)

24

Route 5

(shorter variation 3¼ miles)

Camelford

Outline   Camelford ~ Long Stone ~ Watergate ~ Advent Church ~ Camelford.

Summary   A walk of contrasts from the shelter of the town towards the open Bodmin Moor.

Attractions   Local legend says that this was King Arthur's Camelot (South Cadbury in Somerset is more generally reputed to be Camelot) and that Slaughter Bridge was the site of his last battle.

This walk passes through the town centre of Camelford where there is a park for the children and a relaxing spot by the River Camel for the adults. There are magnificent views from the walk although the route does not reach the open moor. For those who wish to tread the open moor, they may turn north east at Watergate and reach the heights of Little Rough Tor.

The Long Stone is a fascinating object, lean against it and ponder its history, set in this remote spot. Look closely and notice the vein of quartz which runs through it and in the nearby wall notice the vast amount of milky quartz which has been used in its construction.

At Watergate, take a rest by its delightful bridge and notice the quartz grit in the stream bed and the polypods growing on the walls in the vicinity.

No one knows why Advent church got its name. It is mainly 15th century construction with a Norman font dating from the 12th century and carved roof bosses above the porch and the aisles.

A riverside route gives a delightful ending to the walk. Don't forget to visit the North Cornwall Museum opposite the car park at the end of the walk.

Refreshments   There are tea shops and inns in Camelford.

25

Route 5

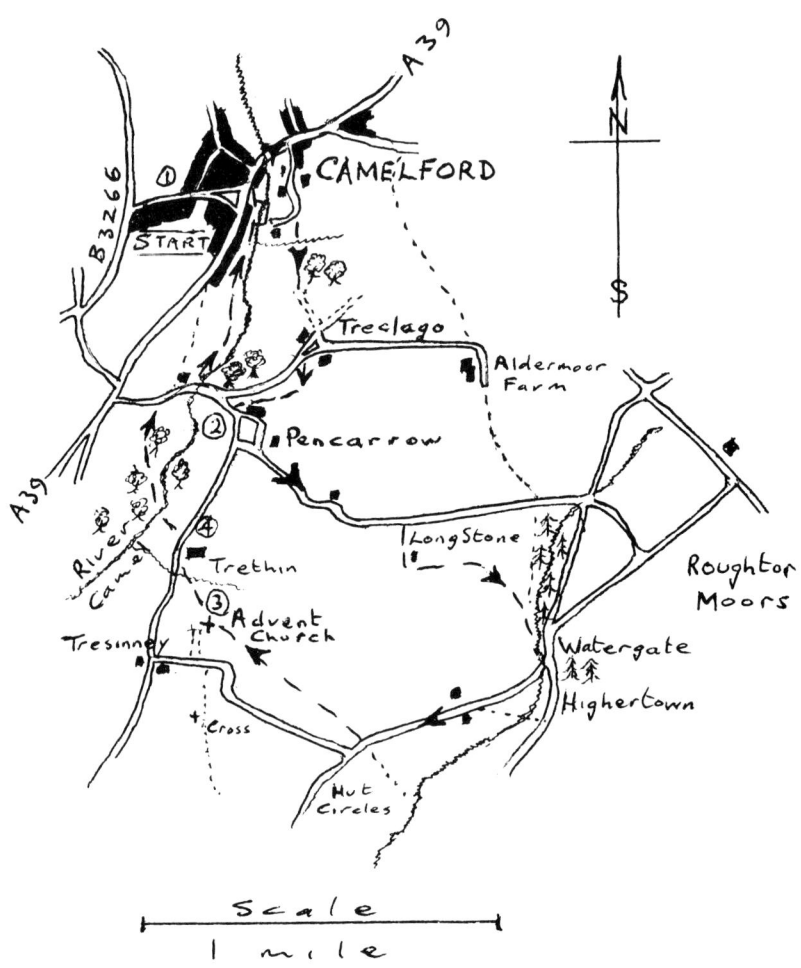

Route 5

5 miles
(shorter variation 3¾ miles)

Camelford

START   At the car park opposite the tourist information office just off the main street (A39) in Camelford (G.R. 104835).

ROUTE

1. *Walk downhill from the car park, turn left along the main street to cross the river, and turn first right into a lane. Follow the lane as it rises with the valley on your right. As the lane starts to descend, cross a stile into the field on the left. Follow the hedge on your right, then bear slightly to the left to cross the bridge over the stream and then go up, through the gate. Maintain the same direction ahead, aiming for the right hand side of the trees, and pass through the gate into the lane. Follow the lane until you reach the tarmac road. Turn right and, after about 100 yards, turn left over a stone stile. Walk down the field, heading towards the distant farm buildings, to cross a very narrow bridge in the valley. Head for the right hand side of the farm buildings and go through a narrow gate.*

2. *Turn left on to the lane. Follow this lane uphill, ignoring any right turns, and about 200 yards beyond an "s" bend look for the stone stile on the right which will lead you to The Long Stone. Beyond The Long Stone, turn left to follow the wall on your right to two gates with a stone stile. Cross the stile and bear slightly right to keep the wall on your right. The wall gives way to a fence on the right. Just before the conifer plantation, turn right over a stile through the wire fence. Walk away from the fence at about a right angle but bearing slightly left, to walk downhill to a stile near a stream at the end of the conifers (Sitka Spruce). Follow the stream on your left towards the road bridge (Watergate) and turn right on reaching the lane. Just before the next road junction, turn right over the stile (note the Church ahead which is our next destination) and walk down the field and towards the right hand hedge. Cross through the hedge at the stile and turn 45 degrees left to reach the gate on the far side of the field. Walk through the gate and down the field with the hedge on your right (the hedge then turns away from you to the right) to find a stile in the middle length of the hedge ahead at the bottom of the field. Cross the stile and head to the church.*

3. *After visiting the church leave by the small kissing gate at the rear of the church and walk down the field with the hedge on your right. Turn right across the stream and head for the left hand side of the buildings, to reach the road. Turn right along the road for a few yards.*

4. *Just beyond the buildings, turn left through the farm gate and walk down the field with the hedge on your left. Bear right to cross the bridge over the stream. Follow the stream to your right briefly but bear away from the stream towards the woods. Enter the woods by the stile. Walk up through the woods to a stone ladder stile, then bear right to keep a level path across the field to the road. Turn right down the road (ignore the footpath sign on the left) and turn left at the river bridge. Follow the river to the town. Turn left up the main street, then right at the top of the hill to the car park.*

SHORTER VARIATION

At point 2 turn left on to the lane, and then immediately turn right to reach point 4. Turn right through the gate to the stream in the valley.

DING DONG MINE (Route 9)

Route 6

(many variations available)

Wadebridge and the Camel Estuary

Outline Wadebridge ~ The old railway line ~ Tregunna ~ Wadebridge.

Summary A flat walk alongside the Camel, then rising to cross farmland but with many options.

Attractions The railway line from Bodmin through Wadebridge to Padstow has been converted into a footpath and cycleway of incomparable interest and variety. At Bodmin one can explore the town, visit the jail, visit Bodmin Steam Railway or explore more of the line as far as Wenfordbridge, or catch a return bus to Wadebridge.

Wadebridge has a number of places to hire cycles if you wish to take the weight off your legs for a time, but beware! The scenery along the estuary is so distracting that you may steer into the water - it's safer to walk!

This walk is just a sample of the many which you can do along the line. It takes in some of the best views of the salt marsh and mud flats where such a wide variety of birds may be seen (or heard). The estuary is the feeding and resting place for many wading birds and wildfowl which breed in the far north in the short summer and then migrate south to avoid the freezing Arctic weather. Some ducks feed on the algae. All year round there are herons, cormorants, oystercatchers, and mute swans.

You could note the number of wild flowers which you see on the walk but there are so many you may be delayed. The moist shale along the cuttings is covered in plants.

A short distance from Wadebridge you will see the field boundary walls made of vertical slabs of slate. Over the far side of the estuary you may see boats under construction, being repaired or cast in glass fibre in moulds.

Refreshments Wadebridge, Bodmin, Padstow, offer a variety of cafés, restaurants and inns.

Route 6

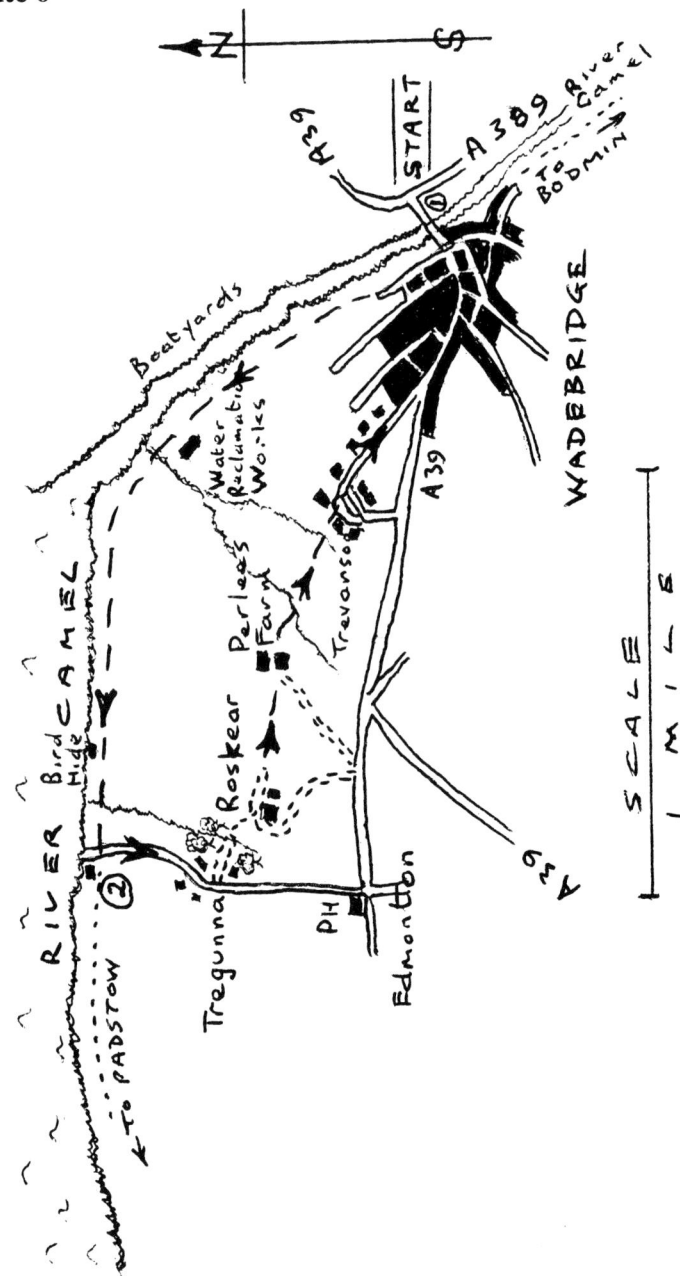

30

Route 6
3½ miles
(many variations available)
Wadebridge and the Camel Estuary

START *At the bridge over the River Camel in Wadebridge. (G.R. 991722). There are several places to park nearby.*

ROUTE

1. *Walk from the bridge towards the town and turn right at the traffic lights into Eddystone Road. Walk along the road and continue ahead at the end through the gates on to the estuary walk. After about 1½ miles, just past the bird hide, take the path which leaves the track on the right to climb up to the bridge above the track.*

2. *Turn left over the bridge and follow the lane for about ¼ mile to a group of houses. Bear left and left again (with houses on your left) to enter a narrow lane with a house then on your right. Follow the lane to the end and descend, bearing right to the stream. Cross the stream and bear slightly to the right towards the farmhouse ahead to walk with the hedge on your right. Turn right through the second gate by the second house, and then left. Pass the small barn on your right and walk along the track and through the gate directly ahead at the end of the track. Bear slightly to the left to cross the field, then cross a stile and bear left slightly to maintain the same direction towards another stile. Climb the stile and pass through the farmyard with the barn on your left and then through the right hand gate on to the track which leads down to the stream. Beyond the stream bear left to walk above but about 50 yards away from the stream to cross the next stile. Maintain a similar direction but further from the stream and cross the stile in the wire fence. Head for the farm buildings ahead and cross the stream over a small bridge. Climb uphill and head for the left hand end of the bungalow to cross the stile. Walk with the barn on your left and then along the tarmac road. Take the second turning on the left (just beyond the post box) and follow this lane as it bends to the right. Follow this lane to meet the main road, then follow the main road ahead to return to the bridge over the Camel at the start point.*

ALTERNATIVE ROUTES.

There are several alternatives along this disused line. You may continue to Padstow and take the direct route, or detour around the inlet on the left to Little Petherick. The same circuits can be approached from Padstow.

C   31

BRONZE AGE CARVING (Route 4)

Route 7

(shorter variation 3½ miles)

Perranporth and Wheal Francis

Outline Perranporth ~ Bolingey ~ Caer Kief ~ Wheal Francis ~ Perranzabuloe ~ Bolingey ~ Perranporth.

Summary A delightful walk passing through some forgotten backwaters of Perranwell where the railway is overgrown, the mines are disused, and nature has returned to surprise you.

Attractions The quiet narrow lanes between Perranporth and Perranwell are a strange contrast to the noise of the surfing beach of the bustling resort. Part of the route is parallel with the disused railway and the area between is a haven for wildlife. There are two ancient hill forts near the route and at the highest points there are panoramic views of the surrounding country with the inevitable derelict mine chimney, and in other places views to the rolling surf of Perranporth.

After Caer Kief there is an optional diversion to Ventongimps passing through a wood full of interesting flora; but where you may get your feet "damp".

Perranporth itself is full of diversions of a different kind but you may prefer to sit on the cliff at Droskyn Point and watch the activity from your vantage point.

The vast sand dunes of Perranporth drifted and submerged two churches dedicated to St. Piran. The first, built in the 6th or 7th century was "discovered" in 1835. It contained three headless skeletons. An old cross now marks the site of the second church, built in the 12th century and abandoned in the 15th. Nearby, a large ampitheatre, St. Piran's Round, is worth a visit.

Refreshments There is a wide selection of cáfes, restaurants and hotels in Perranporth.

33

Route 7

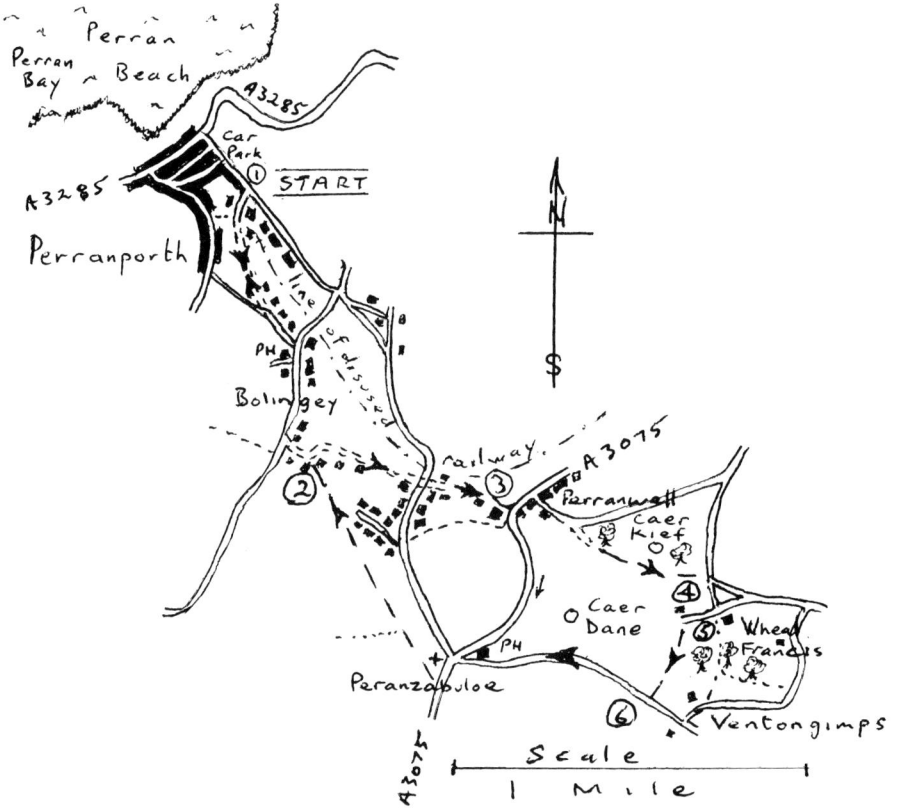

Route 7   5 miles

(shorter variation 3½ miles)

Perranporth and Wheal Francis

START   *From the large car park opposite the Fire Station (just off the main street (B3285) in Perranporth) in Station Road.*

ROUTE

1. *From the Fire Station, walk away from the sea up Station Road and after 250 yards turn right, still on Station Road, to pass between the stone buttresses of a former railway bridge. Do not enter the industrial estate but go ahead up the track. Walk uphill to meet a tarmac lane and carry on downhill. Turn right at the bottom of the hill to enter Bolingey. Pass the Bolingey Inn and, after the trout farm, turn left over the stream bridge and walk along the lane.*

2. *Bear left (note your return route on the right) and follow the track to meet the next tarmac road. Cross this road to follow the track opposite and eventually join the main road (A3075).*

3. *Follow the main road ahead (do not turn right uphill unless following the short route). Turn right at the converted chapel along and up the narrow lane. After 150 yards the road bends to the left but take the path straight ahead. Follow it as it becomes a field path and continue with the wood on your left (Caer Kief). Maintain the same direction straight ahead to meet the lane.*

4. *(At this point the actual site of Wheal Francis lies straight ahead and down a road to the right). At the lane turn right downhill and then right again to pass a cottage.*

5. *Carry straight on past the cottage. (If you wish to divert into the wood to see the flora then turn left at the cottage). At the bottom of the lane bear left into the field to walk with the house garden boundary on your immediate right. Beyond the house turn left and cross the bridge over the stream. Follow the path ahead to the road.*

6. *Turn right on to the road and walk to the main road junction by the church. Turn left and then right to walk the path alongside the churchyard. Walk ahead up the track and maintain the same direction (north west) when entering the open field. From the crest of the field head for the gap ahead. Maintain this same direction until you reach the bottom of the fields. Turn through the gate on the right and follow the worn path ahead to reach the lane (although the official path appears to turn left at the gate and pass through the yard of the house). You are now at point 2, so bear left along the lane to the road. Turn right, pass*

35

Bolingey Inn and turn left. Where the lane bears left go straight ahead along the track used on your outward journey and retrace your steps to the car park.

SHORTER VARIATION

At point 3 turn right and follow the main road, then turn right on to the path beyond the church mentioned in 6 above.

A QUAINT CORNER OF MOUSEHOLE

Route 8

(shorter variation 4 miles)

Mousehole and Lamorna Cove

Outline Mousehole Harbour ~ coast path ~ Lamorna Cove ~ Raginnis Farm ~ Mousehole.

Summary A beautiful cliff top walk to a delightful cove.

Attractions Mousehole is a very quaint little Cornish fishing village clustered around the harbour. The cliff tops afford panoramic views of this delightful coastline. There is plenty of scrub, woodland, streams, and old quarries en-route to occupy the interest of the children, not to mention the obvious delights of a break at Lamorna Cove and a visit to the harbour and beach at the end of the walk at Mousehole.

At the end of the walk, nearby, you can visit the Merry Maidens and the Pipers standing stones, or the Minnack Theatre at nearby Porthcurno, which was also the starting point for the undersea cable route to Australia.

Above Mousehole is the grave of Dolly Pentreath who died in 1777 and is said to be the last person to speak Cornish as her native tongue.

The Merry Maidens stones are maidens who were turned to stone for dancing on Sunday - according to legend.

Refreshments There is plenty of choice for refreshments at Mousehole.

MOUSEHOLE HARBOUR

37

Route 8

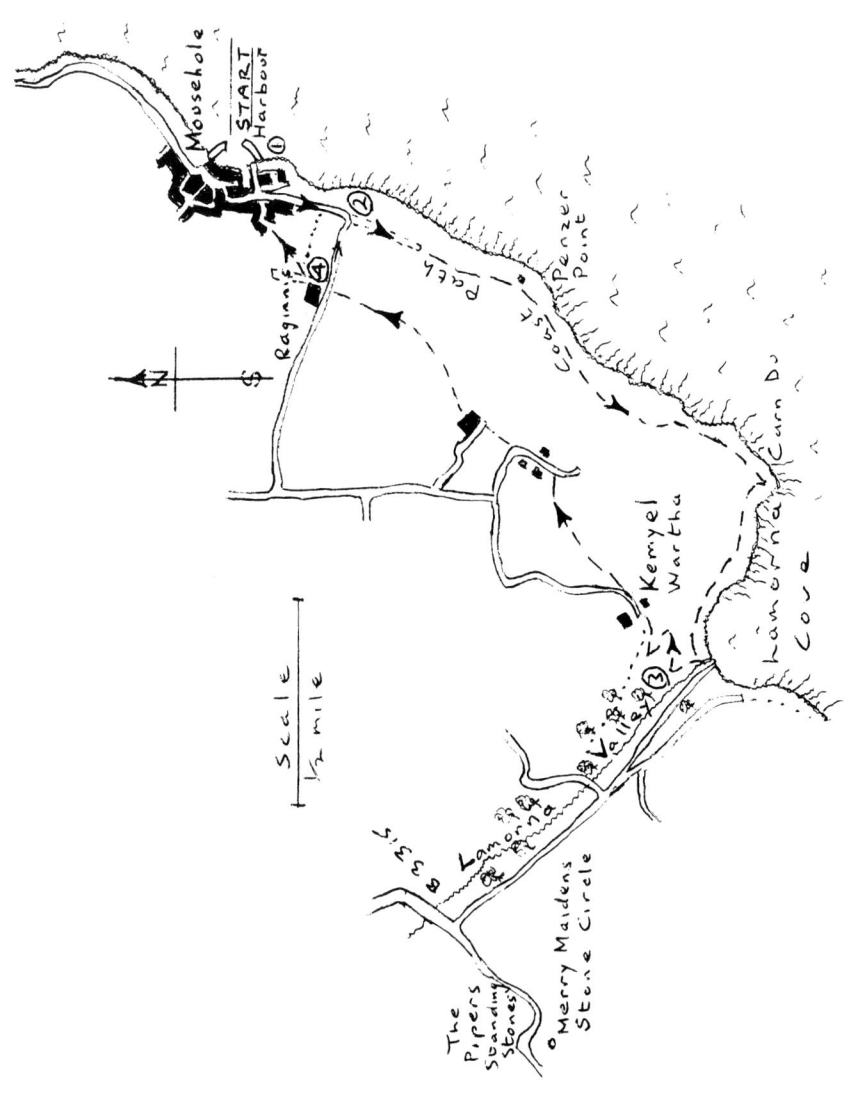

Route 8

5 miles

(shorter variation 4 miles)

Mousehole and Lamorna Cove

START *From the south harbour arm at Mousehole (G.R. 470263). There is a small car park at this point but in the busy season it would be advisable to park outside the village centre by following the direction signs on the approach road from Newlyn.*

ROUTE

1. *Walk away from the village centre, following the road, with the sea on your left. Continue along this road as it turns right at the end. Walk uphill to the next junction (Merlin Place), then up the narrow alley ahead. Turn left on to the main coast road. Follow this coast road as it climbs on the cliff edge for about ½ mile.*

2. *Where the road turns right and heads inland, follow the track ahead, which is signed as the coast path, until you reach Lamorna.*

3. *At the beach toilets at Lamorna the coast path meets a path heading inland alongside the stream. Follow this latter path as it turns uphill, then continue to follow it as it turns left then right at the old quarry. At the top of the cliff turn right where a signpost indicates a path joining from the left. Join the farm drive, follow it as it bears left, and walk beyond the farm. Climb the stile on the right and walk along the field path, beside the hedge. When the next farm buildings come into view deflect slightly to the right to cross the stile on to the farm track. Maintain the same direction along the track to reach the road and, just before the road turns left, take the stile on your right and follow the path to your left. The path opens out to a grassy area adjoining a road on approaching the next farm buildings. Bear left here to cross the stile which leads to a path passing between the outbuildings of the farm. Follow the path to Raginnis Farm. Cross the stile to join the road.*

4. *At Raginnis Farm keep the farm on your left and walk towards the end of the track. Cross the stile on your right and bear left to walk towards the next two gates, your course being slightly downhill towards the sea. (Look closely below the gates and you may find stone steps set in the bank). Maintain this direction and cross the stile on to a narrow lane. Cross the lane and follow the path which leads downhill to meet the road. Turn right at Cuckoo Cottage, downhill, and then right again at the bottom to return to the harbour arm.*

SHORTER VARIATION
Walk from Lamorna Cove to point 4 then turn right to follow the road downhill to the coast. Where the road turns left, you turn right to follow the coast path to return to Lamorna Cove.

TREGESEAL CIRCLE, WITH DOWSERS

Route 9
14 miles
(shorter variations 2¾ and 7 miles)
Quoits Circles and Mines

Outline   Men an Tol ∼ Nine Maidens ∼ Chun Castle ∼ Chun Quoit ∼ Carn Kenidjack ∼ Tregeseal Stone Circle ∼ St. Just ∼ Geevor Tin Mine ∼ Pendeen ∼ Wheal Ball Hill.

Summary   A walk through Cornwall's past ranging from the Prehistoric to the Industrial Revolution. **This is a walk which can be split into several sections and done on separate days.**

Attractions   In this area of Cornwall known as Penwith there is a fascinating collection of prehistoric sites including stone circles, quoits, fogous, standing stones and castles. In many parts the field pattern, surrounded by stone walls with huge stones at the base, has remained unchanged since the Iron Age. This walk takes in several of these sites and others can be visited by minor extensions of the circuit.

Along the coast there are many reminders of the mining activities that once prospered in this area. At Pendeen visitors may go underground to see the Geevor Tin Mine.

A compass may be useful on the open moorland, especially in misty weather.

In St. Just is the Plain-an-Gwarry, a theatre that was used for miracle plays in the Cornish language in mediaeval times. The church includes part of a building erected in 1336 and the Selus Stone, 1 metre high, carries a Roman inscription and a Greek monogram.

Near Pendeen another popular attraction is the lighthouse and beach, and also the Bottallack Engine Houses, near the cliffs.

Holed stones such as Men-an-Tol are associated with traditions of healing or fertility. Men Scryfa commemorates the death of an Iron Age warrior, while Chun Castle is a fine Iron Age hill fort.

Refreshments   There are cafes and inns at St. Just and Pendeen including one at the Geevor Mine. There are cafes at Trewellard.

NOTES - *There is another fogou about ½ mile further along the coast path north of Geevor Mine. Lanyon Quoit lies about 1 mile south east along the road from point 1. Carn Euny is near Sancreed which lies 3 miles south east of St. Just.*
Madron Well and Baptistry is about 4 miles from the start of the walk.
The Carn Gloose Barrow at Cape Cornwall can be visited by using a short diversion west of St. Just.

Route 9

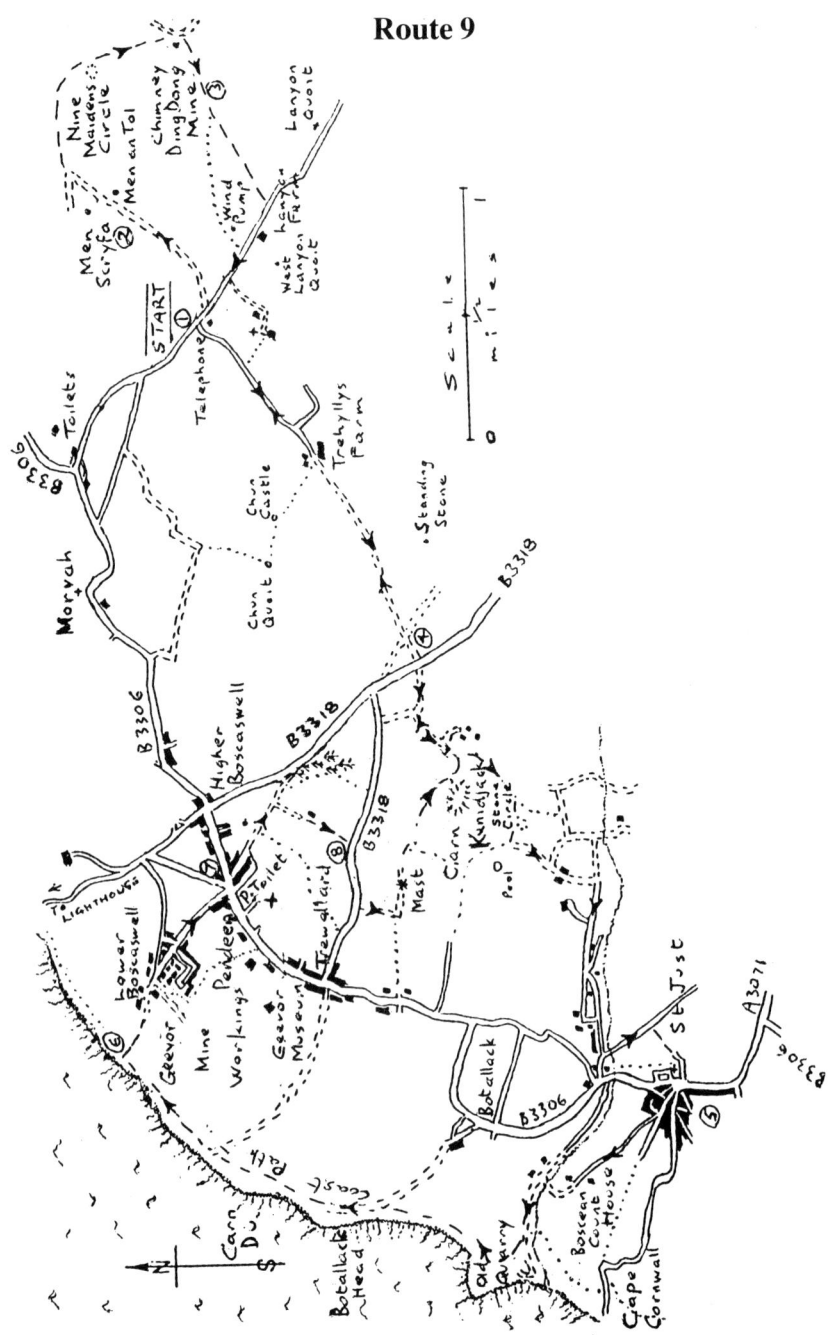

Route 9

14 miles

Quoits Circles and Mines

START   *From the telephone kiosk on the unclassified road which leads off the coast road B3306 St. Ives/St. Just about ½ mile north east of Morvah (the direction sign at the junction indicates "Madron and Penzance"). There is space to park at the roadside which is just less than a mile from the coast road. (G.R. 418344).*

ROUTE

1. *Walk south east (i.e. in the direction away from the coast road) for a few yards and turn left to walk north east along the broad track signed to Men an Tol. After about ½ mile take the stile on the right to Men an Tol.*

2. *Return to the path and turn right to pass Men Scryfa standing stone on the left. Where the track opens out from its boundary walls, follow the track as it goes ahead bearing to the right. At the Nine Maidens stone circle continue in generally the same direction but bearing slightly right to head for the distant chimney. On reaching the chimney turn right to pass through a gate into the enclosed moorland and follow the path ahead to the next gate/stile.*

3. *At the next gate/stile bear slightly to the left to reach the track ahead leading to the road. Turn right at the road and return to the start point.*

Stage 2

Turn left (At pt. 1) and follow the lane to Trehyllys Farm. Follow the farm track as it bears right through the farm buildings, then bear slightly left to join the track between two walls which heads to Carn Kenidjack, the rocky outcrop on the distant horizon. (To visit Chun Castle and Quoit turn right after the farm buildings and walk uphill on the open moor). Follow the track towards Carn Kenidjack for about 1 mile to the road.

N.B. - *Along this section take careful note of the distant features including Chun Quoit, the aerial on the hill on the left which looks like a flying saucer, and the standing stone on the left. Note the path which joins from the right just before the road, and the track which crosses. These will be valuable markers for the return journey.*

4. *Cross the road and continue towards Carn Kenidjack along the track. Note the tracks from right and then from left, and particularly note the nine electricity cables carried generally on three poles but at this point there are four poles adjoining the track. When the track reaches open moor and the walls turn away, take the path on the left, keeping the Carn on your right. Follow the path downhill to the stone circle. Turn right at*

43

the circle and walk about 100 yards, then turn left to follow a track with walls on both sides which leads away from the open moor. Continue past a track which joins on the left and turn right at the next "T" junction, where the track meets a narrow lane. Walk downhill on the lane and turn left at the main road. After 200 yards take the footpath to the right to St. Just church.

5. *From St. Just church walk to the clocktower and down the narrow alley just beyond the clocktower called Boswedden Road. Follow this across the crossroads and later fork right to pass Boscean Count House, following the track to the stream. Over the bridge turn left with the stream on your left. Ignore the left fork downhill and then ignore the right fork uphill. Instead follow the track to the cliffs but turn right just after the coast path joins from the left, to follow the coast path for about 2 miles to Geevor Tin Mine at Pendeen.*

6. *At the far end of the slurry lagoon of the mine turn right up the path where the coast path turns left. Follow the path uphill to the road junction. Take the road ahead (on the right) to the crossroads at the main road (B3306).*

7. *Walk uphill with the car park/toilets on your right, bear left to a road junction, turn right and reach open country. 300 yards beyond the junction turn right along the track with walls on both sides and maintain this direction to reach the next tarmac road.*

8. *Turn right and follow the road. After 200 yards, where two tracks leave the road on the left, take the right hand track. Turn left along the track to the high transmission mast. Maintain the same direction beyond the mast across open moor to reach the outcrop of rocks in the distance (Carn Kenidjack).*

Bear left at Carn Kenidjack passing the Carn on your right and heading for the four poles supporting the electricity lines. Join the track (passing the group of four poles) and go straight ahead to point 4.

Cross the road and maintain the same direction following the track ahead. Avoid the track which forks off to the left and pass Trehyllys Farm to follow the road straight ahead to reach the starting point.

SHORTER VARIATIONS

A. *Start at point 1 and complete the circuit of points 1, 2, 3 and back to 1.*

B. *Start at point 4 and complete the circuit 4, 5, 6, 7, 8, 4.*

A further alternative is to start at either St. Just point 5 and finish at Pendeen point 7 or vice versa and return by bus to the start. The road between St. Just and Pendeen is very busy in summer and is not recommended for walking.

Route 10
5¼ miles
(shorter variation 2 miles)

Loe Pool

Outline Car Park ~ Degibna ~ Loe Bar ~ Penrose House ~ The Causeway ~ Degibna ~ Car Park.

Summary A mainly level walk except for the short stretch from the car park. By approaching from the alternative car parks at Helston or Porthleven any uphill work can be avoided.

Attractions Loe Pool is a large freshwater lake where the water is held back from the sea by a bank of shingle. The walk around The Loe offers variety and fascination for all.

You will recall the story of King Arthur's sword Excalibur which was thrown into the water after his death only to reappear in the hand of the Lady of the Lake and this walk is around the reputed site of the event, although Dozmary Pool on Bodmin Moor is also reputed to hold this honour. Helston is most famous for the annual Furry Dance around the town on Flora Day in May. Helston was once a port but is now severed from the sea by the bar.

Due to this barrier Helston is sometimes flooded by the river and from time to time the shingle is removed to allow water levels to subside. The area has been designated as a site of special scientific interest and on the west side of the lake is a bird hide. Due to the varying nature of the site from marsh at the north to open sea at the south, there is a wide variety of flora. On the west side of The Loe are some Monterey cypress and on the opposite bank, some majestic Monterey pines. Castle Wary, the site of which is at the north end of the walk, was a silver mine. Much of this walk is on National Trust property open from dawn to dusk without charge.

After the walk, nearby you can visit the Royal Navy Air Station at Culdrose, Flambard's Theme Park, and the Folk Museum in Helston.

Refreshments There is a wide variety of refreshments at Helston and Porthleven.

Route 10

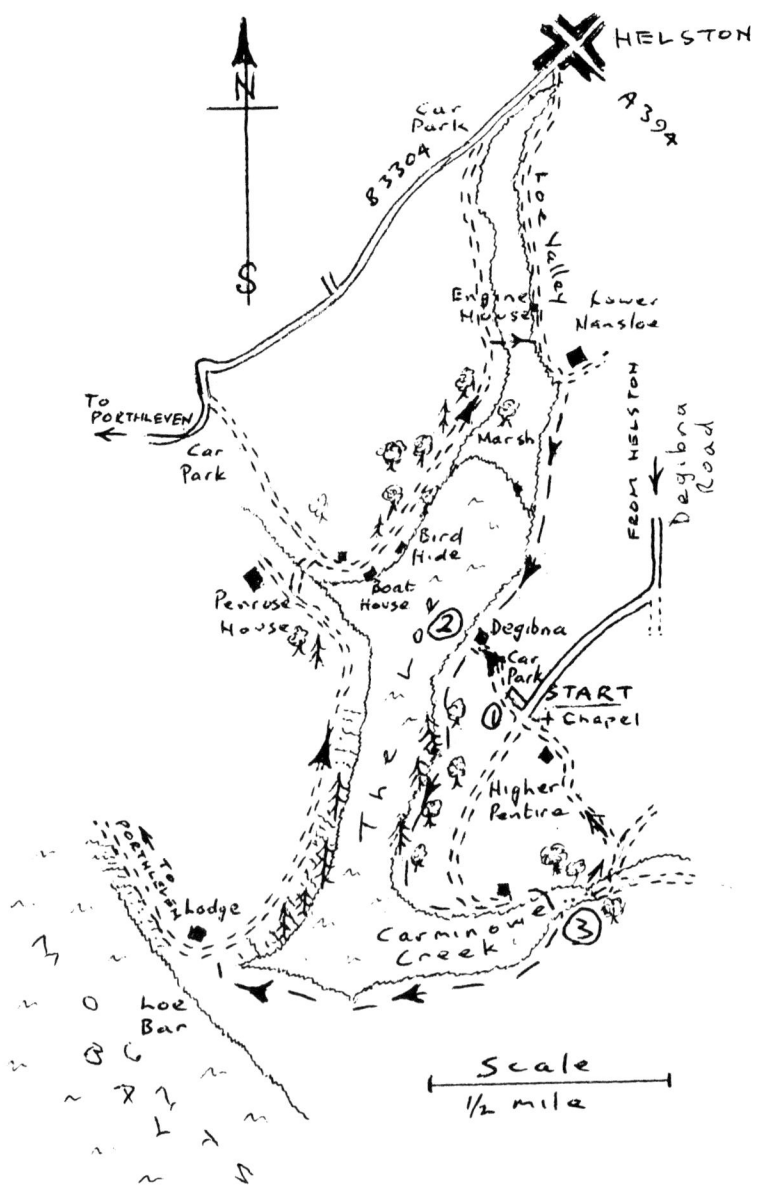

Route 10

5½ miles
(shorter variation 2 miles)

Loe Pool

START *From the National Trust Car Park between Higher Pentire Farm and Degibna (G.R. 653251). Take the narrow lane which leads south west off the A394 a few yards north west of the junction of the A394 and A3083 (adjoining Culdrose Airfield, Helston), to reach Degibna.*

ROUTE

1. *Walk to the end of the car park away from the entrance and follow the track down to the water.*

2. *Turn left to follow the water's edge of The Loe. (Note the nearby landmarks at this point for your return journey. The boat house on the opposite shore is a useful marker). Follow the path as it rounds the headland and turns back up Carminowe Creek.*

3. *At the top of the creek turn right to follow the edge of Carminowe Creek to the Loe Bar at the sea. Walk across Loe Bar to the lodge and turn sharp right to follow the west side of The Loe. Follow the path as it completes a U turn near Penrose House then pass the boat house and bird hide. About ½ mile beyond the boathouse turn right through a gate which leads across a causeway through the marsh. Cross the bridge and turn right along the main path alongside the marsh and then along the shore of The Loe. At point 2 turn left to return up the path to the car park.*

SHORTER VARIATION

At point 3 go straight ahead over the stile into the woodland and follow the track. Turn left, then take the lefthand fork to pass Higher Pentire Farm and return to the car park.

NOTE

Alternatively you may approach the walk using car parks which are available at:

1. *Helston adjoining Penrose Amenity Area on the B3304.*
2. *Porthleven at the start of the coast path.*
3. *Near the entrance to Penrose Park off the B3304 between Helston and Porthleven.*

THE GIANT'S QUOIT

Route 11

Coverack, St. Keverne and Porthoustock

Outline   Coverack ~ Boscarnon ~ Trevalsoe ~ St. Keverne ~ Porthoustock ~ coast path ~ Coverack.

Summary   A pleasant country ramble starting with a short uphill climb followed by the undulations of the coast path.

Attractions   Many visitors to Coverack are there to study the interesting geological formations along the coast. A hard rock, serpentine, forms the core of much of the Lizard peninsula. Formerly used for some decorative building work, it is now made into souvenirs. The red, green and purple of the cliffs at nearby Kynance Cove are derived from the serpentine which also surrounds many caves.

The walk passes through a variety of scenery including woodland, open country, quarries, and shore line. There are plenty of spots for hide and seek in the woods, streamside, diversions in the valley, or picnics on the cliff.

Porthoustock is a favourite launching place for divers visiting the notorious Manacles Rocks, a mile offshore where many ships have foundered. 400 victims of shipwrecks on the rocks are commemorated in St. Keverne church, the spire of which was rebuilt as a landmark for shipping.

After the walk you can visit the Goonhilly Earth Station (Satellite Communications) nearby. At the Lizard the lighthouse may be open if the foghorn is not sounding.

Refreshments   At Coverack there is a hotel and a cafe for refreshments. At St. Keverne there is an inn but the restaurant at Porthoustock opens only on certain evenings.

A few yards to the right at point 2 you will find a farm specialising in ice cream and fudge.

Route 11

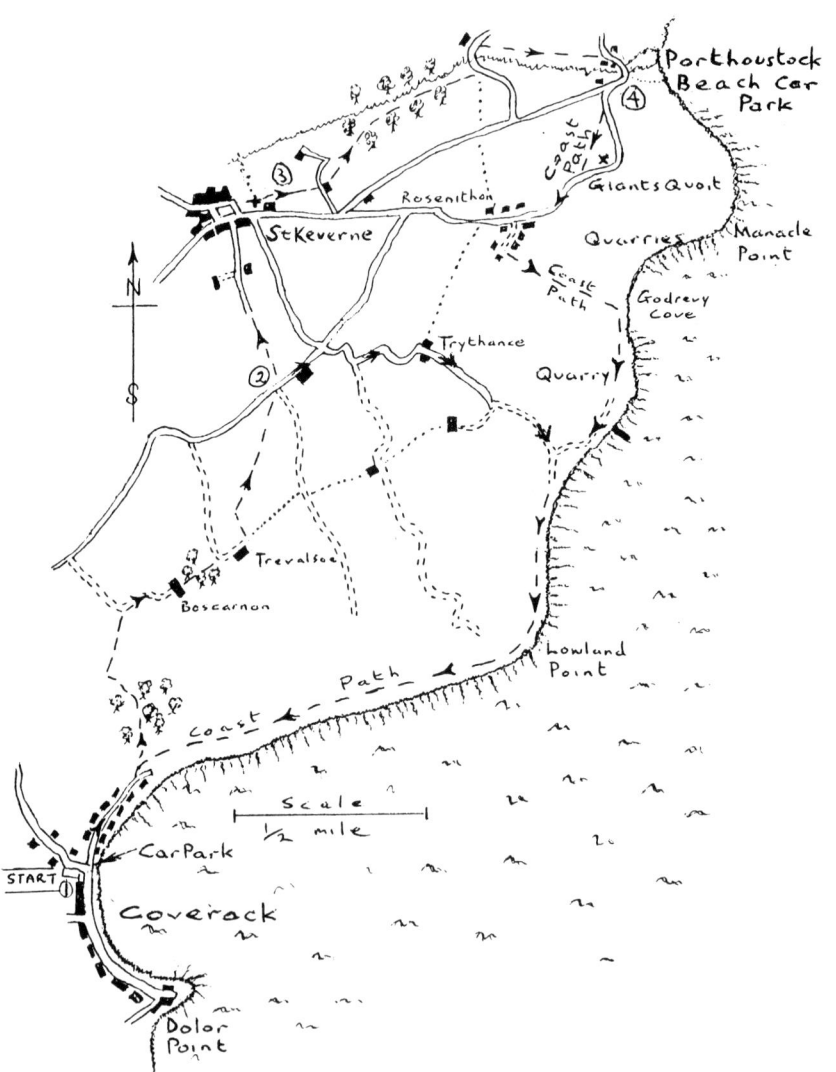

Porthoustock
Beach Car
Park

Coast Path

④

Giants Quoit

Rosenithon

③

St Keverne

Manacle
Point

Quarries

Coast
Path

Godrevy
Cove

Trythance

②

Quarry

Coast
Path

Trevalsoe

Boscarnon

Lowland
Point

Path

Coast

Scale
½ mile

Car Park

START ①

Coverack

Dolor
Point

N
S

Route 11 (shorter variation 5 miles) **6½ miles**

Coverack, St. Keverne and Porthoustock

START   *From the car park at the north end of the sea front at Coverack. (G.R. 782186).*

ROUTE

1. *Walk from the car park towards the sea and turn left to follow the narrow lane which runs parallel with the coast. At the end of the houses take the path which forks off to the left. Continue climbing uphill until the path levels out and enters a small clearing of grassland. A narrow track with stone walls on both sides leads from this area of grass. Follow this path as it bears left to leave the woodland and the walls finish. Continue along the track with hedges on both sides for about 100 yards to the junction, and turn right into the field to follow the hedge on your left. Maintain this same direction to reach a stile leading on to a lane. Carry on ahead in the same direction along this lane to Boscarnon Farm and beyond to reach Trevalsoe Farm. Beyond this farm turn left over the stile and walk with the hedge on your right. Keep the same direction as the hedge drops away on the right to reach a stile. Follow the hedge on your right, but where the hedge turns right just bear half right across the field to the stile. Keep the next hedge on your right to reach the next stile, then follow the next hedge on your left to the next stile. Maintain the same direction across the next field to reach the road.*

2. *Cross the road, and over the stile bear slightly right to walk diagonally across the field to the corner, then walk with the hedge on your right through two fields to reach the road. Carry straight ahead along the road to the centre of St. Keverne.*

3. *From the village square, walk into the churchyard, bearing left then right, to leave at the far end and follow the path downhill. Cross the road and keep the same direction down the valley. Turn left, uphill, for a few yards at the next road and then right to resume the same direction down the valley to Porthoustock.*

4. *Bear right at Porthoustock to walk up the steep road leading away from the village. Take the first road turning on the left, and after a few yards cross the stile on your right (signed as the Coast Path). Bear half left across the field and continue (past the Giant's Quoits) to the road. Bear right along the road and at the next hamlet (Rosenithon) turn left down the narrow lane which becomes a track. Bearing left, enter the field and follow this Coast Path to return to Coverack, keeping to the signed path through the quarry.*

51

SHORTER VARIATION

At point 2 do not cross the road but bear right on to the road. Turn right at the next junction, then left, passing Trythance, to reach the Coast Path. Turn right to walk to Coverack.

ST. KEVERNE

Route 12   5½ miles

St. Mawes and St. Just in Roseland

Outline   St. Mawes Harbour ~ Castle ~ Carrick Roads ~ St. Just ~ Garage ~ Percuil ~ Harbour.

Summary   There is plenty of sailing activity at St. Mawes and the walk should give you the opportunity to rest awhile and study the action. It can be very exciting watching from the castle across Carrick Roads as dinghies and yachts vie with the open sea or retreat back into the harbour. In rough weather you can watch the ferry struggling across from Falmouth. Carrick Roads is a deep water anchorage and many ships anchor here while being repaired or when they are awaiting their next commission, or even awaiting the breakers' yard. Nowadays you may see a drilling rig amongst the ships.

Why not visit the castle en-route? It has been described as Henry the Eighth's most decorative fort and has gardens stretching down to the sea. There are plenty of opportunities to break the journey and relax or play on the beach.

The churchyard at St. Just in Roseland is a fascinating place and a leaflet is available at the lych gate to explain the details and what to look for.

Alongside the main path are 55 stones, each engraved with a text. The grounds contain the usual variety of flora but also have plants brought from all over the world and many sub-tropical plants which thrive in this mild climate next to the sea. Before you leave see if you can find St. Just's holy well and spring.

Refreshments   There is a wide choice of cafes and hotels or restaurants in St. Mawes; and light refreshments at St. Just.

Route 12

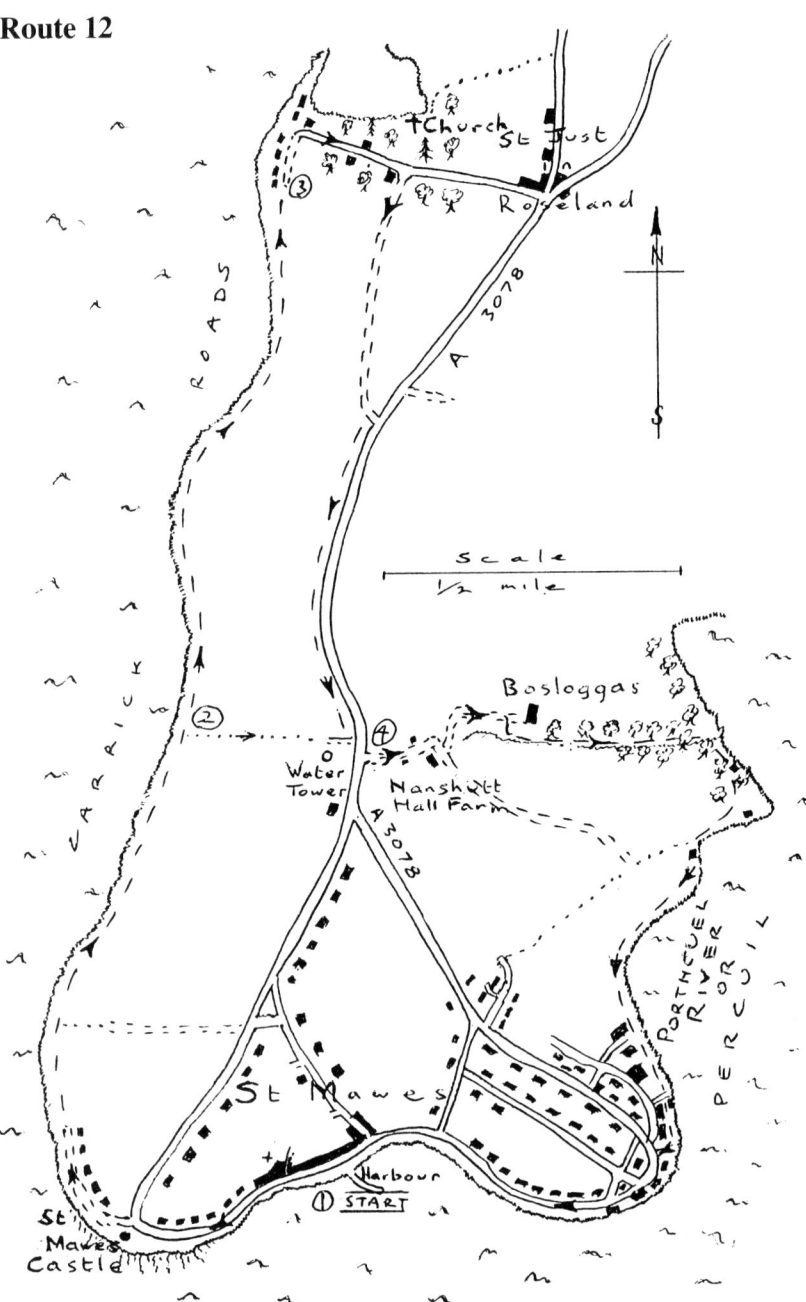

St Just

Church

Roseland

A 3078

N

S

ROADS

scale
½ mile

Bosloggas

②

④

Water
Tower

Nanshutt
Hall Farm

A 3078

St Mawes

PORTHCUEL RIVER or PERCUIL

+

Harbour

① START

St
Mawes
Castle

③

VARRICK

Route 12

5½ miles
(shorter variation 4¾ miles)

St. Mawes and St. Just in Roseland

START   *At St. Mawes harbour (G.R. 848330); there is a car park nearby which is signed from the main road approaching St. Mawes.*

ROUTE

1. *Walk along the sea front towards the open sea (i.e. westwards), and at the Castle take the lane which continues along the sea front. At the end of this narrow lane carry on through the field ahead for about ¾ mile.*

2. *Here there is a path to the beach, a stile and a direction sign which points ahead to St. Just 1 mile, and a path to St. Mawes Garage. Continue along the coast to St. Just.*

3. *At St. Just join the lane and follow it as it bends right. At the church lych gate bear right up the track. At the main road cross the stile on your right to walk with the main road on your left to the water tower and join the road.*

4. *On the road turn right, then left down the track. Turn right through the gate at the second house, then follow the track as it bends left and right to reach the boundary of Bosloggas. Turn right to the stream, then left to follow the stream to the shore. Turn right and follow the path above the estuary passing two buildings on your left but the third will be on your right. Follow the estuary path to the boatyard. Turn right up the drive for a few yards, then left, and follow this path to the next boatyard. Turn right up the drive to the main road and turn left and follow the road to the harbour.*

SHORTER VARIATIONS

A. *At point 2 go ahead a few yards, turn right through the hedge and immediately left to follow the narrow path to the water tower at point 4.*

B. *At point 4 turn right and follow the path to point 2. Turn left and retrace your steps to the harbour.*

NOTE

The route passes the entrance to the church where you may collect an explanatory leaflet. However, if you wish to avoid additional climbing you may enter the grounds by following the foreshore beyond point 3 and looking for the path on your right.

N.B. - *At the time of publication the route between point 4 and the river is obstructed at Nanshutt Hall Farm and the County Council are taking legal action. Pending this action walkers must use the alternative path ½ mile south along the A3078. This starts at the end of Percuil View on the Polvarth Estate.*

MERLIN'S CAVE (Route 4)

Route 13

6 miles
(longer variation 10 miles)

Mevagissey

Outline   Mevagissey ~ Penwarne ~ Gorran Churchtown ~ Gorran Haven ~ Chapel Point ~ Portmellon ~ Mevagissey.

Summary   An undulating walk through the Cornish countryside and coast.

Attractions   The walk gives a small glimpse of the colourful old fishing port of Mevagissey at close quarters and then offers a grand panorama of the port from the higher ground of the coast path including views of the magnificent cliffs along the coast. There are many tempting bays to rest, paddle or indulge in beach games with picnic spots here or on top of the cliffs.

West Bodruggan Nature Reserve is a very quiet spot where the woodland runs down to meet the marshy ground and pool along the valley bottom and where you should pause and be quiet for a while. The buzzard which normally wheels high in the sky may screech just above your head if you disturb it here, or if you are late in the day you may listen to the owls' hooting chorus.

Caerhays Castle is a splendid sight from the hilltop above Porthluney Cove. It was designed by John Nash in the Gothic Style. The gardens are occasionally open to the public. Allow four to five hours to complete the 10 mile walk. The road between Gorran Churchtown and Gorran Haven can be very busy in summer.

The Parish church of Saint Goran incorporates some Norman remnants although there is no trace of anything from Saint Goran's original structure dating six hundred years before the Normans. The embattled south porch was rebuilt in the 16th century and inside the church there is a Norman font and many ancient carved bench ends.

Those taking the short route will find St. Goran's Adventure Playground between Churchtown and Gorran Haven.

Refreshments   Mevagissey has a very large choice of refreshments and Gorran Haven has some. There is a small beach cafe at Porthluney Cove and a public house at Gorran Churchtown.

Route 13

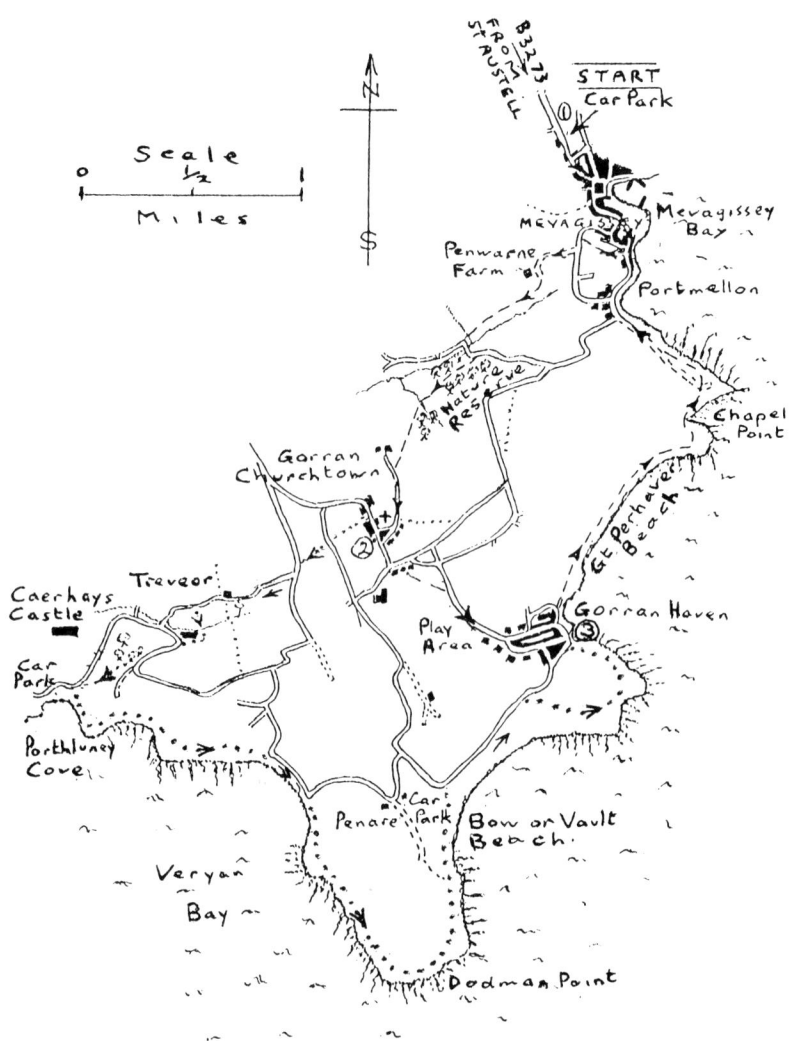

Route 13
6 miles
(longer variation 10 miles)
Mevagissey

START *At the main car park adjoining the main road B3273 into Mevagissey. (G.R. 014450).*

ROUTE

1. *Walk towards the sea along the continuation of the main road B3273 (but against the traffic flow in this one way street). At the next junction, a small sign on the Ship Inn says "Market Square" although it hardly looks like one. Turn right here up Fore Street and follow this road for about ½ mile. Turn right into Penwarne Lane and at the top, where it meets the tarmac road turn left down the road and then after a few yards, right. Follow the lane as it bears left past Penwarne Farm and take the gate ahead on the right. Follow the path as it bends to the right following the contours on a level above the stream on your left. Follow the path as it drops to the stream at the end of the fields to cross a branch of the stream using the footbridge ahead. Turn left on the road, cross the main valley stream, bear left uphill for a few yards then turn right into the nature reserve. At the end of the wood turn right down towards the stream and then left to leave the wood. Walk across the field with the stream on your right to cross another branch of the stream ahead over the culvert. Maintain the same direction to walk uphill with the wood on your left then bear left to follow the wood again on your left but bearing slightly away to cross the stile at the top of the field. Maintain the same direction and, when the church comes into view, head slightly to the right of the church, keeping the farm buildings away to your right. Cross the stile which leads on to the lane and bear left along the lane to the church. Bear right around the church to the main road at Gorran Churchtown.*

2. *Turn left and follow the main road downhill and up, then around the lefthand bend. Turn right along the public footpath signed to Gorran Haven and then follow the road downhill, taking the right fork to reach the sea and point 3.*

3. *Turn left along the main street parallel with the beach at Gorran Haven. Take the right hand turn to walk along the street nearest to the sea and walk up Cliff Road. After a short distance turn right along the narrow lane and then follow the coast path to reach the coast road at Portmellon. Follow the coast road to Mevagissey and turn left at the Ship Inn to return to the car park.*

LONGER VARIATION

From point 2 turn right along the main road at the church for 100 yards, then turn left at the post box just beyond the public house car park. Cross the gate/stile and walk ahead with the hedge on your right. Maintain this direction beyond the end of the hedge line to reach a stile alongside the second lane. Turn left and immediately right along the lane. Pass the farm at Treveor (with footpaths left and right and a pool). 250 yards further cross the stile into the field on the left and walk down to the bridge over the stream. Bear right and follow the fence of the houses to the lane. Follow the lane in front of the houses and maintain the same direction along the road until it bends sharply to the left. Here, ignore the track ahead and enter the wood on the right. Again maintain the same direction and cross the stile to leave the wood. Head for the castle when it comes into view to reach the stile on to the road and then the beach.

Recross the stile back into the field again and climb the hill, keeping the fence and the cliff on your right. Follow the coast path to Hemmick Beach and then to Gorran Haven. At Gorran Haven turn right down the main street to point 3.

BODINNICK

Route 14
6 miles
(shorter variations 4 and 2½ miles)

Polruan and Bodinnick

Outline   Polruan Ferry ~ Pont Pill ~ Bodinnick Ferry ~ Hall Walk ~ Polruan Church ~ Pencarrow Car Park ~ Lantic Bay ~ Polruan Ferry.

Summary   A walk with a lot of ups and downs if you take in both ferry points but well worth it for splendid scenery and contrasts. The start from Pencarrow car park can cut out both ferry points if you wish to minimise climbing.

Attractions   Ferry landing piers make a fascinating interlude on the walk which passes through the typically Cornish villages of Polruan and Bodinnick.

The open cliff tops above Lantic Bay offer a magnificent view of the sea and coast and present opportunities for picnics and kite flying, if you can resist the temptation to rush down to the glorious beach. The land is owned by the National Trust and they control the scrub to encourage the smaller plants such as dovesfoot cranesbill, squills, bluebells and primroses although many butterflies thrive in the remaining gorse and brambles.

The estuary is lined with deciduous woodland and offers a very pleasant sheltered walk when the coast path is swept by wind. At Hall Walk above Bodinnick King Charles narrowly escaped death when a shot killed a man standing near to him during the Civil War in 1644. The granite monument on Hall Walk relates to the author Sir Arthur Quiller Couch. Below Hall Walk you will generally see a variety of large ships in the dock at Fowey or awaiting their turn to load with china clay. There are the ruins of two forts on the side of the harbour at Fowey and in olden times, a chain was stretched between the two to protect the town from hostile ships.

Refreshments   There is a tea shop and a public house at Polruan, an inn at Bodinnick, and a wide choice of refreshments at Fowey.

Route 14

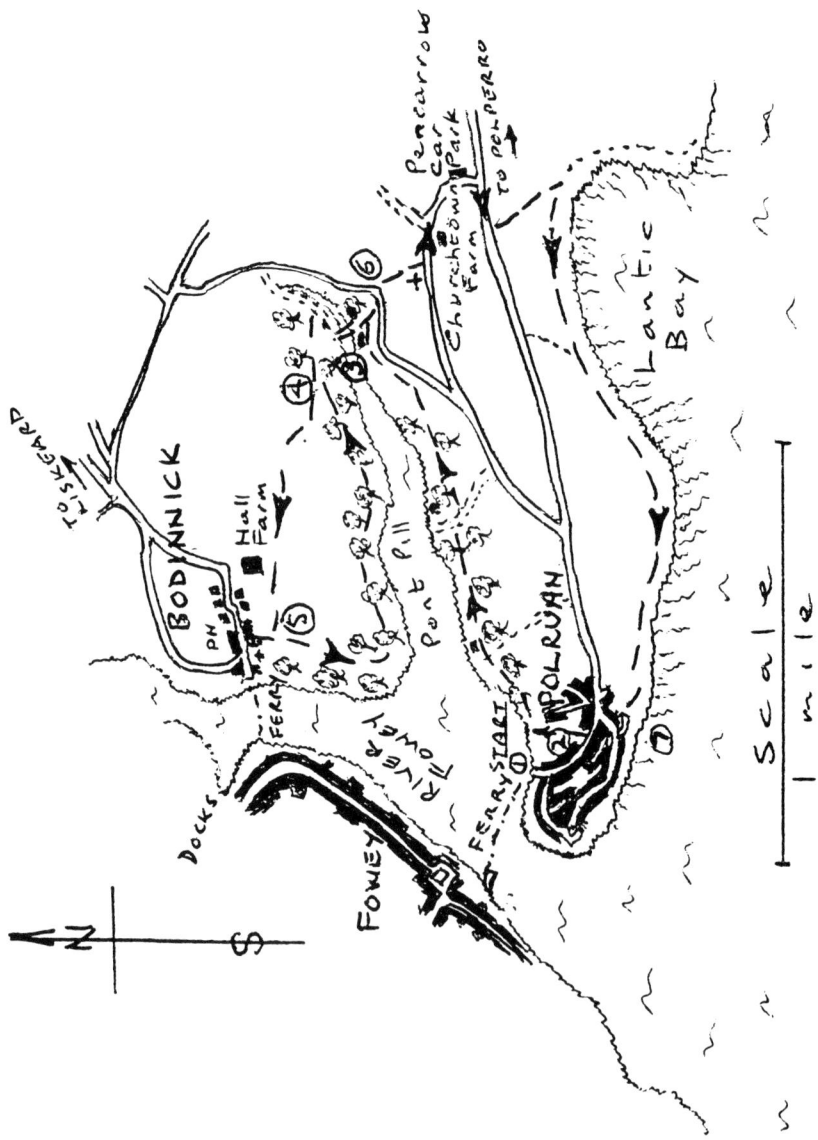

Route 14   6 miles

Polruan and Bodinnick

START   *From the Fowey Ferry landing at Polruan. (G.R. 126510).*

ROUTE

1. *Walk from the ferry up the main street ahead for about 300 yards.*

2. *Turn left up the steps and along the path adjacent to house number 73. Bear left where the path turns downhill and follow this path along the estuary (avoiding any paths which run downhill left to the waters edge). After ½ mile bear right and immediately left to cross a tarmac drive and continue alongside the estuary. Where the footpath meets the road do not join the road but carry on along the path through the National Trust land with the road hedge on your right. Continue until you meet another path which runs steeply to your left to the bridge over the estuary.*

3. *Cross the bridge and bear right uphill along the path, then take the first turn left to climb up through the wood.*

4. *On crossing the stile to leave the wood bear slightly to the left to climb up the field to a gate. Pass through the gate and walk ahead with the hedge on your right. When you meet two gates together after about 500 yards, take the right hand gate to walk down the track towards the farm. Walk straight ahead at the farm, keeping the same direction, with the barn on your right. Join the path along the estuary at the war memorial.*

5. *Turn left at the memorial to continue the walk (or right to visit the ferry at Bodinnick). Follow the path along the estuary to return to point 4, walk down through the wood and turn right to point 3. *From the bridge at point 3 walk up the path through the wood which was the original route from Polruan but now continue to the top to meet the tarmac road. Bear left downhill and turn right through the right hand gate of the two gates.*

6. *Walk uphill and turn left on to the road at the church. Follow the road uphill and as it bears to the right to reach the car park beyond Churchtown Farm, which is Pencarrow Car Park. Turn right at the road junction just past the car park, then after 100 yards turn left at the stile. Walk across the field with the hedge on your left to reach the coast path and turn right. After about a mile the path meets the road.*

7. *Turn right on to the road and follow it as it bears to the left to meet the main road. Turn left down the main road hill to the ferry at Polruan.*

E   63

SHORTER VARIATIONS

A *At point 3 do not cross the bridge but turn around and follow the route from point 3 to point 6 and then to 7, using the directions following the asterisk in 5 above.*

B *The shortest circuit starts at point 5, follows the estuary to the bridge at point 3 then returns across the hill to point 5. This may be joined by those using the Bodinnick ferry and walking uphill past the public house and the church to turn right at Hall Walk Cottage.*

Car parking is available in Polruan (G.R. 123507) and before reaching Polruan at Pencarrow Car Park G.R. 149513) and at (G.R. 158517). There are car parks in Fowey. In main season all are rather busy.

LOOE

64

Route 15
3 miles
(shorter variation 2½ miles)

Looe and Kilminorth Woods

Outline   Looe ~ Kilminorth Woods ~ Kilminorth Farm ~ Riverside ~ Looe.

Summary   A lovely woodland and riverside walk. The steep section at the early stage can be modified to suit by taking side paths if so desired.

Attractions   Looe is a traditional fishing port with narrow streets generally bustling with holiday makers in the season. Houses are perched precariously on the steep hillside flanking the river but this walk rises up the steep hillside away from the bustle of the town. It combines the delights of the sessile oak woodlands, with the pleasure of farmland and the attractions of the small beaches and salt marshes along the river. The saltmarsh attracts many wading birds including dunlins, oyster catchers and also curlew with their distinctive call and curved bill.

As the walk passes through the different types of habitat there is a very wide variety of mosses, wild flowers and ferns along the route. There are masses of wild garlic along the road in the woods and thrift growing on the salt marsh. As there are no sheep in the woods you may be able to pick some bilberries en-route.

The 16th century Guildhall is now a museum.

Refreshments   There is a wide choice of refreshments in Looe.

MEN SCRYFA (Route 9)

Route 15

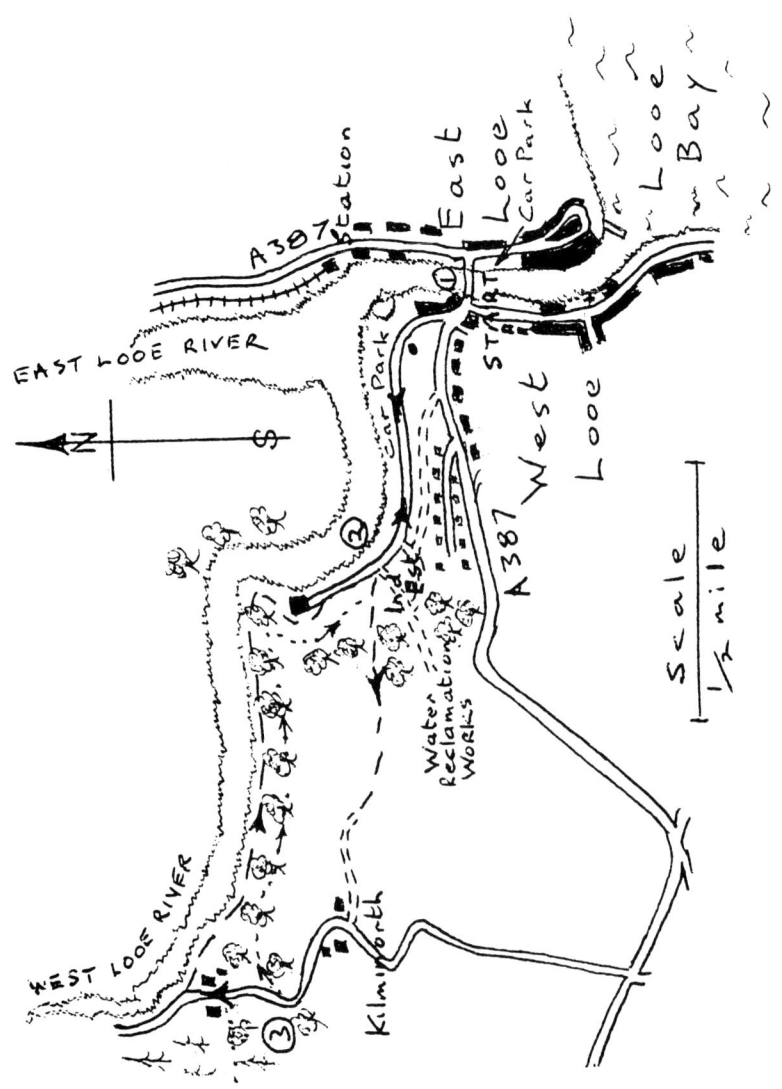

Route 15
3 miles
(shorter variation 2½ miles)
Looe and Kilminorth Woods

START *From the A387 road bridge over the river in Looe. (G.R. 254536). There are a number of car parks in Looe adjoining the River but they can be busy in high season. An alternative is to park at the railway station in Liskeard (follow signs from the main road A38) and take the train down the valley following the East Looe River to Looe.*

ROUTE

1. *On the bridge, face away from the sea, walk towards the left hand bank of the river, then bear right at the end of the bridge to walk along the west bank, up river, past the large car park.*

2. *Beyond the small industrial estate on the left, and near the end of the car park, a gate on the left and a stile lead into the South West Water reclamation works. Do not take this stile but take the footpath nearby on the right of the stile which rises up a steep ridge line into the woods. Maintain this direction ignoring any paths to either side which lead off this ridge line. Shortly, you pass through an earth bank and, still on the same direction, follow the bank for a short distance to emerge from the woods on to open farmland. Walk diagonally across the field again in the same direction, following the slight ridge line (now less pronounced). When two gates come into view, head for the right hand one and similarly, in the next distant hedge, head for the right hand gate, still maintaining virtually the same direction which you followed from the start of the initial climb. Turn right at this second hedge to walk downhill for a few yards on a track and follow this as it then swings to the left. At Kilminorth Farm turn right to leave the track and follow the tarmac road downhill.*

3. *Shortly after the road enters the woods a broad track leads into the woods on the right hand side and is the shorter variation. Follow the tarmac road downhill for the main route and where it meets the river turn right to follow the bankside path to Looe. (Note that just before the boatyard the path will lead you on to the foreshore. If you do not wish to walk on the foreshore, or if the tide is in, then retreat into the woods a few yards and take the branch path which leads behind the boatyard).*

SHORTER VARIATION

At point 3 take the wide gate on the right of the road, follow the path to reach the river and continue to Looe.

Those who wish to avoid climbing all the way to the top of the woods on the first stage will find several side paths which offer short walks through the woods at a lower level.

KING DONIERT'S STONE

Route 16

(shorter alternative 2 miles)

Siblyback Reservoir and King Doniert's Stone

Outline   A circular walk mainly on tarmac but with options to take to the footpaths.

Summary   An interesting foray at the southern edge of Bodmin Moor to see a waterfall at a National Nature Reserve, a reservoir and an ancient monument.

Attractions   In the compact area to the south of the Siblyback Reservoir there are several spots worth visiting. Where you park and how you accomplish the circuit will depend on which parts interest you most, and how busy the traffic and parking is at the reservoir.

The reservoir has many attractions at the recreation area including craft for hire and tuition. There is a shop and refreshments.

The dam is a grand sight with its great mass holding back the weight of water while the excess cascades over the spillway and rushes into the River Fowey below, to dash over the Golitha Falls about 1½ miles downstream.

King Doniert ordered a huge stone to be erected for the good of his soul in the 9th century, even if you are not greatly interested in stones and such things it is worth a visit if only for the view.

The Nature Conservancy Council have laid out two or three walks to visit the Golitha Falls and the Nature Reserve.

While you are in this part of Bodmin Moor there are many other points of interest in the vicinity. To the north west is Jamaica Inn, Bolventor, and Dozmary Pool. The pool is where King Arthur ordered Sir Bevidere to throw Excalibur into the water although legends also award this distinction to other lakes. Colliford Lake lies in the same direction, and with the Loveney Nature Reserve, welcomes fishermen, birdwatchers, and walkers. To the north east lies the Hurlers stone circles and the distinctive outcrop of rock known as The Cheesewring.

Refreshments   Refreshments are available at the reservoir recreation area.

Route 16

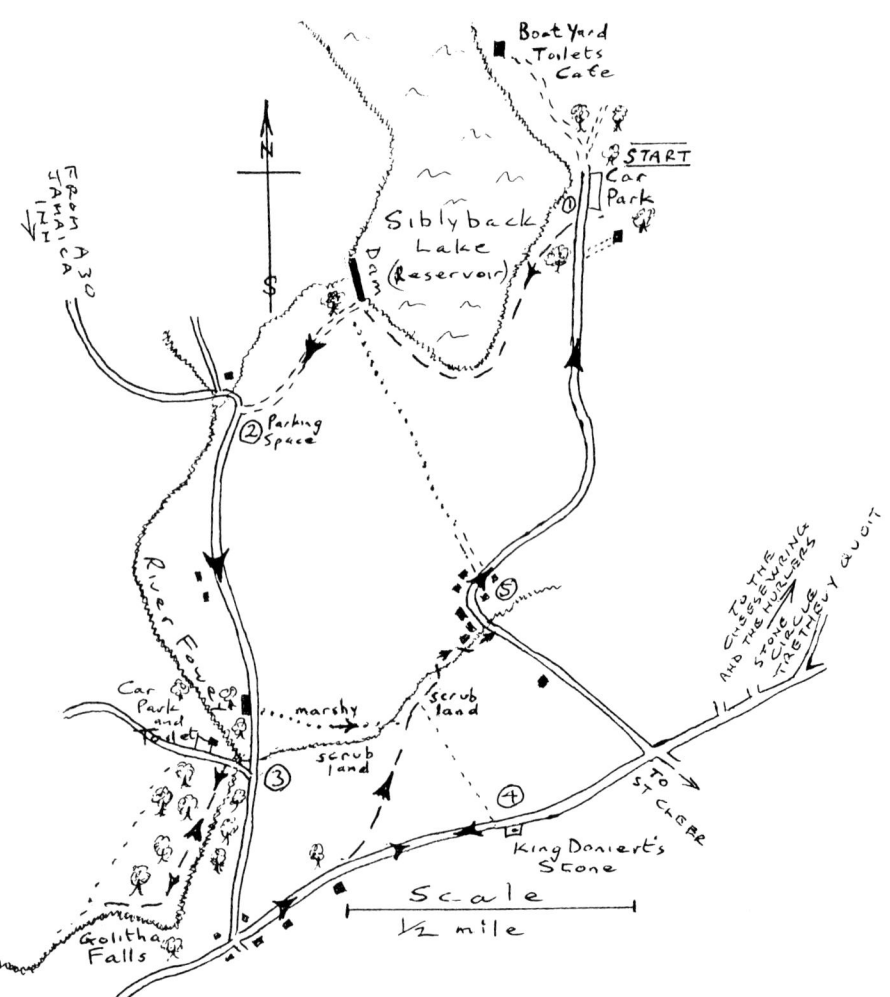

Route 16   3 miles
(shorter variation 2 miles)
Siblyback Reservoir and King Doniert's Stone

START   *From the car park at the recreation area at Siblyback Reservoir. (G.R. 237706).*

ROUTE

1. *Walk back from the car park in the direction from which you came and bear right along the path at the edge of the reservoir to the dam. From the dam follow the road down to the public road at the entrance gate of the water company's property.*

2. *Turn left along the road. Continue along the road for about ¾ mile. Note the small terrace of cottages on the right and a gate and public footpath sign on your left just before a road on your right.*

3. *Turn right along this road to the car park for Golitha Falls. Turn left and follow the river to the falls. Return to the road and turn right, then go over the river and turn right again, at point 3. After 400 yards turn sharp left at the road junction to walk to King Doniert's Stone, taking note of the public footpath which leads off to the left between two hedges and also the path which passes through the first of a pair of gates on the left just before the stone.*

4. *From the stone return to the first of the two footpaths which you had noted and turn right to walk between the two hedges. Maintain the same direction in the field with a hedge on your left. The path from the Stone joins your path on your right and, shortly after this point, the path becomes ill-defined as it enters bushes. Do not be tempted to follow the path which curves to the left but maintain virtually the same direction as before through the bushes to emerge with the stream on your immediate left. At this point you are walking against the flow of the stream and heading upstream. If you are walking downstream then retrace your steps and try again. Follow the stream, now on your right to the buildings ahead and cross the stream just before the farm to join the road with the stream on your left.*

5. *Turn left and follow the road as it bends sharp right. Follow the road to the reservoir start point.*

SHORTER VARIATION

When walking from point 2, turn left through the gate opposite the row of cottages at the roadside just before point 3. The path is undefined and marshy. Basically you must follow the stream until you meet the road at point 5. A close inspection of the stream bank will reveal a gate where you cross the stream and pass through the bushes to emerge in the field. Here, turn left, pass through a hedge, and turn left on the main route. After a few yards you will see the path joining on your right from King Doniert's Stone. Follow the instructions above in 4 "the path becomes ill-defined as it enters bushes" etc.

NOTE

Although I have described a circular route, consult the map and you will notice that there are several variations available to suit your requirements. Traffic and parking conditions on busy days may dictate which of the possibilities are most practicable. This may also depend on the ages of the party and whether they can tackle the marshy section of the route.

SIBLYBACK RESERVOIR

Appendices

TOURIST INFORMATION CENTRES
* indicates open all year.
Bodmin — Shire House, Mount Folly Square. Tel. 0208 76616.*
Bude — Crescent Car Park. Tel. 0288 354240.
Camelford — North Cornwall Museum, The Cleave. Tel. 0840 212954.
Cornwall Tourist Board, Old County Hall, Station Road, Truro, TR1 1BR. Tel. 0872 74282.*
Falmouth — 47 Killigrew Street. Tel. 0326 312300.*
Fowey — Post Office, Custom House Hill. Tel. 072 683 3616.*
Hayle — A30 Southern Cross Self Serve, Loggans Moor. Tel. 0736 755485.
Laity — Lizard and Helston T.I.C., near Wendron. Tel. 0326 40899.*
Launceston — Market House Arcade, Market Street. Tel. 0566 772321.*

Looe — The Guildhall, Fore Street, East Looe. Tel. 05036 2072.
Lostwithiel — Community Centre, Liddicoat Road. Tel. 0208 872207.*
Newquay — Cliff Road. Tel. 0637 871345.*
Penzance — Station Road. Tel. 0736 62207.*
St. Ives — The Guildhall, Street an Pol. Tel. 0736 796297.*
Tideford — A38 Heskyn Hill, near Saltash. Tel. 075538 397.
Truro — Municipal Buildings, Boscawen St. Tel. 0872 74555.*
Victoria — A30 near Roache. Tel. 0726 890481.
Wadebridge — Town Hall. Tel. 020 881 3725.
West Country Tourist Board, P.O. Box 73, Exeter, EX1 1RJ. Tel. 0392 76351.*
Cornwall is such a large area that details of all wet weather and other attractions would take up too much space and also be out of date too soon. The following is a list of the main attractions of family interest. Details of current prices and opening times may be obtained from the nearest tourist information office or the telephone numbers below. Places marked with an asterisk * are open all year round.

NATIONAL TRUST PROPERTIES
The Trust owns and protects many properties in the area and many of the walks pass over their land. You will enjoy using their facilities and I hope that you will support them financially, by offering assistance in their working parties, or otherwise. The vast amount of open space which they maintain for free access by the public is too large to list. Some of the main houses/gardens are:
Antony House, Torpoint. April to end Oct. Tue., Wed., Thu. and B.H. Mon. (and in June, July, Aug. on Sun.).
Cotehele, St. Dominick, Saltash. Open end March-End October daily except Fri. (open Good Friday). Garden open daily all year.
Egyptian House, Chapel St., Penzance. Open all year, not Sun. (closed Sun. and Wed. in winter).
Glendurgan Garden, near Falmouth. Open March to end Oct. Tue. to Sat. and B.H. Mon. (closed Good Fri.).
Lanhydrock, Bodmin. Open end March to end Oct. daily (on Mon. garden only open).
Lawrence House, Castle St., Launceston. Used as town museum. April to Mid. Oct.
Saint Michael's Mount, Marazion. Open all year but no regular ferry Nov.-Mar. Normally open only Mon.-Fri. but open some weekends for charities.
Tintagel Old Post Office. Open end March to end Oct. daily.
Trelissick Garden, Feock, near Truro. Open March to end Oct. daily.
Trengwainton Garden, near Penzance. Open March to end Oct., Wed. to Sat. (also B.H. Mon. and Good Fri.).
Trerice, near Newquay. Open end Mar.-end Oct. daily except Tue.
The Trust have preserved the beam engines at Pool, near Redruth which are available for inspection end March-end October, daily. Also the Trust are restoring the Levant Beam Engine, the oldest in Cornwall, at Pendeen.
Full details annually in the National Trust Handbook. The regional office for Cornwall is at Lanhydrock, Bodmin, PL30 4DE. Tel. 0208 74281.

MUSEUMS AND PLACES OF HISTORIC INTEREST
***Altarnum Church,** (the Cathedral of the Moors) and nearby is St. Nonna's Well and Wesley's Cottage at Trewint.
***Boscawen Un Stone Circle.**
***Carn Euny Iron Age Village.**

74

*Chysauster Ancient Village, Gulval, near Penzance. (English Heritage). Tel. 0736 61889.

*Chun Castle and Cromlech, Morvah, near Penzance.

*County Museum and Art Gallery, River St., Truro. Tel. 0872 72205.

Duke of Cornwall's Light Infantry Regimental Museum, The Keep, Bodmin. Tel. 0203 72810.

*Falmouth Maritime Museum, Custom House Quay, Falmouth. Tel. 0326 250507.

*Hurlers Stone Circle and Trethevy Quoit near St. Clear.

Jamaica Inn Museum (Daphne du Maurier Museum).

Potters Museum of Curiosity, Tel. 0566 86838.

*Lanyon Quoit, near Penzance.

Launceston Castle, Launceston. (English Heritage).

*Madron Well and Baptistry, near Penzance.

Maritime Museum, Chapel St., Penzance. Tel. 0736 62476.

*Men Scryfa, Madron, near Penzance.

*Merry Maidens stone circle, near Newlyn.

Mount Edgcumbe House (and Country Park,) Torpoint. Tel. 0752 822236.

*Nine Maidens Stone Circle, near Penzance.

North Cornwall Museum and Gallery, The Clease, Camelford. Tel. 0840 212954.

Pencarrow, House and Gardens, Washaway, near Bodmin. Tel. 020884 369.

*Pendennis Castle, Falmouth. (English Heritage). Tel. 0326 316594.

Penlee House Museum and Art Gallery, off Morrab Rd., Penzance. Tel. 0736 2625.

Penryn Town Hall and Museum.

Restormel Castle, Restormel near Lostwithiel. (English Heritage). Tel. 020887 2687.

*St. Catherine's Castle, near Fowey. (English Heritage).

*St. Clether Well, near Launceston.

*St. Germans Church (and Almshouses).

*St. Keyne Well, St. Keyne.

*St. Mawes Castle, St. Mawes, near Truro. (English Heritage). Tel. 0326 270526.

Perranzabuloe Folk Museum, Ponsmere Rd., Perranporth.

Prideaux Place, Padstow. Tel. 0841 532945.

*Roche Rock (with St. Michael's Chapel Ruins), near Roche.

*Tintagel Castle, Tintagel. (English Heritage). Tel. 0840 770328.

Trelowarren House and Craft Centre, Mawgan in Meneage, Lizard. Tel. 032 622 366.

Trinity House National Lighthouse Centre, Wharf Rd., Penzance. Tel. 0736 60077.

*Warbstow Bury, near Launceston.

Wayside Museum, Zennor. Tel. 0736 796945.

Wheal Martin China Clay Museum, Carthew, St. Austell. Tel. 0726 850362.

OTHER ATTRACTIONS

Automobilia, Motor Museum, St. Austell. Tel. 0726 823092.

Barbara Hepworth Museum, St. Ives. Tel. 0736 796226.

Barbican Aquarium Penzance Harbour.

*Blue Lagoon Leisure, Cliff Rd., Newquay. Tel. 0637 850741.

*Bodmin Indoor Tennis/Sports Centre, Lostwithiel Rd., Bodmin. Tel. 0208 75715.

Bodmin Steam Railway, Bodmin. Tel. 0208 73666.

Bodmin Gaol, Cardell Road, Bodmin. Tel. 0208 76292.

Brass Rubbing Centre, High St., St. Ives. Tel. 0736 793628.

Butter Market Museum, Church St., Helston. Tel. 0326 564027.

Butterfly World and Falconry Centre, Fraddam, near Hayle. Tel. 0736 850 859.

Cycle Hire (for Camel Trail), Bodmin Trading Co., Bodmin and several at Wadebridge. Also at Truro, Cycles, Kenwyn St., Truro.

*Cambourne School of Mines Geological Museum** and Art Gallery. Tel. 0209 714866.

*Carn Brea Leisure Centre,** Station Rd., Pool, Redruth. Tel. 0209 714766.

Carnglaze Slate Caverns, near St. Neot, Bodmin Moor. Tel. 0579 20251.

Colliford Lake Park, near Bodmin. Tel. 0208 82 469.

*Cornish Seal Sanctuary,** Gweek. Tel. 0326 22361.

Cornish Shire Horse Centre, Tredinnick, Wadebridge. Tel. 0841 540276.

*Delabole Slate Quarries,** Delabole. Tel. 0840 212242.

*Dobwalls Adventure Park** near Liskeard. Tel. 0579 20578.

Flambards, Helston. Tel. 0326 564093.

Frontier City, St. Columb Major near Truro. Tel. 0637 881375.

Geevor Mine, Pendeen, near Penzance. Tel. 0736 788662.

Goonhilly Satellite Earth Station, Goonhilly Downs near Helston. Tel. 0872 45400.

Great Trethew Pleasure Park, Horningtops, Liskeard. Tel. 050 34 663.

Helston Sports Centre, Tel. 0326 563320.

Holywell Bay Leisure Park, Newquay. Tel. 0637 830095.

*Land's End.** Tel. 0736 871501.

Lanreath Folk and Farm Museum near Looe. Tel. 0503 20321.

Lappa Valley Railway and Leisure Park, St. Newlyn East, Newquay. Tel. 0872 510317.

Launceston Steam Railway, near Launceston. Tel. 0566 775665.

Merlin Glass, Barn St., Liskeard. Tel. 0579 42399.

Military Vehicle Museum, Lamanva, near Falmouth. Tel. 0326 72446.

Minack (Open Air) Theatre, Porthcurno. Tel. 0736 810694.

Monkey Sanctuary, near Looe. Tel. 0503 262532.

Motorsport Centre, Blackwater, near Redruth. Tel. 0872 560753.

Merlin's Magic Land, Lelant, St. Ives. Tel. 0736 752885.

*Model Railway Exhibition,** St. Thomas Rd., Launceston. (adjoins Launceston Railway, above).

Newquay Zoo and Leisure Park, Trenance, Newquay. Tel. 0637 850933.

Paul Corin's Magnificent Music Machines near Looe. Tel. 0579 43108.

*Paradise Park,** Hayle. Tel. 0736 753365.

Poldark Mine, Wendron, Helston. Tel. 0326 573173.

Shire Horse Trust and Carriage Museum, Lower Gryllis, Treskillard, Redruth. Tel. 0209 713606.

Splash Leisure Pool, Bude. Tel. 0288 356191.

St. Agnes Leisure Park, near Redruth. Tel. 0872 552793.

Tamar Otter Park, North Petherwin, near Launceston. Tel. 056 685 646.

The Port of Charlestown, St. Austell. Tel. 0726 67955.

Trinity House National Lighthouse Centre, Wharf Rd., Penzance. Tel. 0736 60077.

Tunnels Through Time, Newquay. Tel. 0637 873379.

Waterworld Newquay and Zoo, Newquay. Tel. 0637 850933.

World in Miniature, Goonhavern near Perranporth. Tel. 0872 572828.

*World of Model Railways,** Mevagissey. Tel. 0726 842457.

There is a large number of gardens open to the public and a guide/calendar including details of the Festival of Gardens can be purchased from the Cornwall Garden Society. Many are open under the National Garden scheme.

Not included:- Theatres and Cinemas, Farms, Bird Gardens, Potters and Art Studios/ Galleries.

For a complete change take a day trip to the Isles of Scilly (Boat 0800 373307 or Skybus 0736 787017).

A guide to the many facilities at water parks, reservoirs etc. is produced by South West Water, Leisure Services, Rydon Lane, Exeter, EX2 7HR. Tel. 0392 219666.

Details of sports recreation facilities in the larger resorts should be obtained from the nearest tourist information office.

THE OLD POST OFFICE, TINTAGEL

FAMILY WALKS SERIES

Family Walks in the North Yorkshire Dales. Howard Beck. ISBN 0 907758 52 5.

Family Walks in West Yorkshire. Howard Beck. ISBN 0 907758 43 6.

Family Walks in Three Peaks and Malham. Howard Beck. ISBN 0 907758 42 8.

Family Walks in South Yorkshire. Norman Taylor. ISBN 0 907758 25 8.

Family Walks in the North Wales Borderlands. Gordon Emery. ISBN 0 907758 50 9.

Family Walks in Cheshire. Chris Buckland. ISBN 0 907758 29 0.

Family Walks in the Staffordshire Peak and Potteries. Les Lumsdon. ISBN 0 907758 34 7.

Family Walks in the White Peak. Norman Taylor. ISBN 0 907758 09 6.

Family Walks in the Dark Peak. Norman Taylor. ISBN 0 907758 16 9.

Family Walks in Snowdonia. Laurence Main. ISBN 0 907758 32 0.

Family Walks in Mid Wales. Laurence Main. ISBN 0 907758 27 4.

Family Walks in South Shropshire. Marian Newton. ISBN 0 907758 30 4.

Family Walks in the Teme Valley. Camilla Harrison. ISBN 0 907758 45 2.

Family Walks in Hereford and Worcester. Gordon Ottewell. ISBN 0 907758 20 7.

Family Walks around Cardiff and the Valleys. Gordon Hindess. ISBN 0 907758 54 1.

Family Walks in the Wye Valley. Heather and Jon Hurley. ISBN 0 907758 26 6.

Family Walks around Stratford and Banbury. Gordon Ottewell. ISBN 0 907758 49 5.

Family Walks in the Cotswolds. Gordon Ottewell. ISBN 0 907758 15 0.

Family Walks in South Gloucestershire. Gordon Ottewell. ISBN 0 907758 33 9.

Family Walks in Oxfordshire. Laurence Main. ISBN 0 907758 38 X.

Family Walks around Bristol, Bath and the Mendips. Nigel Vile. ISBN 0 907758 19 3.

Family Walks in Wiltshire. Nigel Vile. ISBN 0 907758 21 5.

Family Walks in Berkshire and North Hampshire. Kathy Sharp. ISBN 0 907758 37 1.

Family Walks on Exmoor and the Quantocks. John Caswell. ISBN 0 907758 46 0.

Family Walks in Mendip, Avalon and Sedgemoor. Nigel Vile. ISBN 0 907758 41 X.

Family Walks in Cornwall. John Caswell. ISBN 0 907758 55 X.

Family Walks on the Isle of Wight. Laurence Main. ISBN 0 907758 56 8.

Family Walks in North West Kent. Clive Cutter. ISBN 0 907758 36 3.

Family Walks in the Weald of Kent and Sussex. Clive and Sally Cutter. ISBN 0 907758 51 7.

The Publishers, D. J. Mitchell and E. G. Power welcome suggestions for further titles in this Series; and will be pleased to consider manuscripts relating to Derbyshire from new or established authors.

Scarthin Books of Cromford are the leading Peak District specialists in secondhand and antiquarian books, and purchase good books, music, maps and photographs at fair and informed valuations.

Contact Dr. D. J. Mitchell by letter, or phone Matlock (0629) 823272.
